Colonial Life

AMERICAN VOICES FROM

Colonial Life

Rebecca Stefoff

BENCHMARK BOOKS

MARSHALL CAVENDISH
NEW YORK

The author gratefully acknowledges permission from Verso Books for reproduction of the letter to the bishop of London from Robin Blackburn, *The Making of New World Slavery,* London and New York: Verso Books, 1997.

Benchmark Books
Marshall Cavendish
99 White Plains Road
Tarrytown, New York 10591-9001
www.marshallcavendish.com

Library of Congress Cataloging-in-Publication Data
Stefoff, Rebecca, 1951–
Colonial life / by Rebecca Stefoff.
p. cm. —(American voices from—
Summary: Presents the history of the British colonies in North America, beginning with the Jamestown settlement, through excerpts from letters, pamphlets, journal entries, and other documents of the time. Includes bibliographical references and index.
ISBN 0-7614-1205-0
1. United States—History—Colonial period, 1600–1775—Sources—Juvenile literature.
2. United States—History—Colonial period, 1600–1775—Juvenile literature.
3. United States—Social life and customs—To 1775—Juvenile literature. [1. United States—History—Colonial period, 1600–1775—Sources. 2. United States—Social life and customs—To 1775—Sources.] I. Title. II. Series.
E162 .S77 2002   973.2—dc21
2002003223

Printed in Italy
1 3 5 6 4 2

Series design and composition by Anne Scatto / PIXEL PRESS
Art research by Rose Corbett Gordon, Mystic C.T.

The photographs in this book are used by permission and through the courtesy of:
Front cover & page 56: The Cheney Family by Anonymous, Gift of Edgar William and Bernice Chrysler Garbisch, Photograph © Board of Trustees, National Gallery or Art, Washington; pages ii, viii, xvi, xx, 6, 8, 10, 12, 15, 18, 20, 22, 25, 33, 34, 36, 39, 42, 45, 46, 53, 64, 69, 72, 75, 76, 79, 81, 84, 86 (left), 86 (right), 89, 92, 94, 96, 97, 101, 105, 113 (top): The Granger Collection, New York; pages xii, 112: Bettmann/Corbis; pages xxii, 2, 28: Hulton Archive/Getty Images; page 113 (bottom): Lee Snider/The Image Works.

ON THE COVER: Portrait of a colonial family, the Cheneys, from the National Gallery of Art in Washington, D.C.

ON THE TITLE PAGE: Artist Edward Hicks's idealized painting of a treaty signing between William Penn, founder of the Pennsylvania colony, and the Indians. This work was painted in the 1830s, some fifty years after the event.

Acknowledgments

The author is deeply grateful to the research services provided by Zachary Harris of C/Z Harris Ltd. Identifying and locating sources for the colonial documents quoted in this book would have been infinitely more difficult without his patient, resourceful, and insightful help.

A Note to the Reader

The pieces of history quoted in this book come from the pens of many different writers, some more educated and polished than others. Several hundred years ago, even educated people used spelling, grammar, and vocabulary words different from those of today. I have tried to explain terms that you might not recognize. Some of the spelling and punctuation you will see in these quotations may seem unusual to you. Ignore the strangeness and look for the meaning that lies beneath. Reading the words of the people who lived history is a window into the past—the closest thing to a time machine that we are ever likely to have.

I hope that these original writings from the American colonies make you want to learn more about the people and events of this fascinating time. When a quote sparks your interest, read more by looking up the source from which it comes. You can also find more information about colonial American life in the books and Websites listed at the back of this book.

One more point: Were the colonies in eastern North America English or British? For the first century of the colonial period they were English. Then, in 1707, England was formally united with Wales, Scotland, and Ireland—the other nations of the British Isles—under the name Great Britain. However, historians sometimes use the terms "Britain" and "British" for the entire colonial period to avoid confusion.

Contents

KNOW all Men by these Presents, That *I Jonathan Badger of Charles Town*

For and in Consideration of the Sum of *One Hundred & Seventy five ___* Current Money to *me* in Hand, paid by *Joseph Vanderhorst of Christ Church Parish of the Province aforesaid ___* Whereof *I ___* do Acknowledge the Receipt, and *my* self therewith Fully and Entirely Satisfied, Have Bargained, Sold, Set over and Delivered, and by these Presents, Do Bargain, Sell, Set over and Deliver unto the said *Joseph Vanderhorst One Negro*

Girl Named Jenny

To have and to hold the said Bargained Premisses with the Appurtenances, to the proper Use and Behoof of *him* the said *Joseph Vanderhorst* Heirs, Executors Administrators and Assigns for Ever. And *I* the said *Jonathan Badger* for *my* self *& my* Executors and Administrators, the said Bargained Premisses, unto the said *Joseph Vanderhorst* Executors and Administrators and Assigns, against all and all manner of Persons shall and will *Warrant*, and Defend for Ever, by these Presents. In Witness whereof, with the Delivery of *the said Negro Named Jenny* have hereunto set *my* Hand and Seal this *Sixteenth* Day of *March* In the *Twenty Second* Year of the Reign of Our Sovereign *George the Second* of Great-Britain, &c. Annoque Domini, *1749*

Signed, Sealed, and Delivered
in Presence of us

Jonathan Badger

Sam: ll Stevns

Vanderhorst

Printed for *Eleazer Phillips* in *Charlestown.*

Primary sources reveal history's shameful side as well as its glorious moments. This document, for example, records the sale of a slave in Charleston, South Carolina, in 1749.

About Primary Sources

What Is a Primary Source?

In the pages that follow, you will be hearing many different "voices" from an early period in America's past. Some of the selections are long while others are short. You'll find many easy to understand at first reading, but some may require several readings. All the selections have one thing in common, however. They are primary sources. This is the name historians give to the bits and pieces of information that make up the record of human existence. Primary sources are important to us because they are the very essence, the core material for all historical investigation. You can call them "history" itself.

Primary sources *are* evidence; they give historians the all-important clues they need to understand the past. Perhaps you have read a detective story in which a sleuth must solve a mystery by piecing together bits of evidence he or she uncovers. The detective makes deductions, or educated guesses based on the evidence, and solves the mystery once all the deductions point in a certain way. Historians work in much the same way. Like detectives, historians analyze the data by careful reading and rereading. After much analysis, historians draw conclusions about an event, a person, or an entire era. Historians may analyze the same evidence and come to different conclusions. This is why there is often sharp disagreement about an event.

Primary sources are also called *documents*—a rather dry word to describe what can be just about anything: an official speech by a government leader, an old map, an act of Congress, a letter worn out from too much handling, an entry hastily scrawled into a diary, a detailed newspaper account of a tragic event, a funny or sad song, a colorful poster, a cartoon, a faded photograph, or someone's eloquent remembrance captured on tape or film.

By examining the following primary sources, you will be taking on the role of historian. Here is your chance to throw yourself into an exciting period of American history—the decades before the American colonies became the independent nation known as the United States. You'll come to know the voices of the men and women who settled an unknown shore and built communities. You'll read the words of Native Americans and government officials, servants and slaves, farmers and rebels.

Our language has changed since those days. The colonial vocabulary contained words that will be unfamiliar to someone living in this century. Even familiar words may have been spelled differently then. Don't be discouraged! Trying to figure out language is exactly the kind of work a historian does. Like a historian, you will end with a deeper, more meaningful understanding of the past.

How to Read a Primary Source

Each document in this book deals with some aspect of life in colonial North America. Some of the documents are from government archives or from the official papers of major historical figures. Others are taken from the letters and diaries that ordinary people wrote or from the pamphlets and newspapers that kept the colonists informed. All of these documents help us to understand what it was like to live in the colonial era that gave birth to the United States.

As you read each document, ask yourself some basic but important questions. Who is writing? Who is the writer's audience? What is the writer's point of view? What is he or she trying to tell that audience? Is the message clearly expressed, or is it stated indirectly? Are the words factual or emotional in tone? These questions help you think objectively about a document.

Some tools have been included with the documents to help you in your historical investigations. Unusual words have been defined near some selections. Thought-provoking questions follow many of the documents. They help focus your reading so you get the most out of the document. As you read each selection, you'll probably come up with many questions of your own. That's great! The work of a historian always leads to many, many questions. Some can be answered; others cannot and require further investigation.

A replica of the *Mayflower*, perhaps the most enduring symbol of America's past

Introduction

COLONIAL AMERICA

The British poet John Masefield once called the arrival of the ship *Mayflower* on the Massachusetts shore in 1620 "the sowing of the seed from which Modern America has grown." But modern America sprang from many seeds—not just the Pilgrims who stepped ashore from the *Mayflower* but also fortune-seeking adventurers, merchants and traders, missionaries, dreamers who wanted to create new kinds of societies in a new world, poor men and women who toiled for years to pay for passage across the Atlantic Ocean, and enslaved Africans brought to America by force. And although the United States was born from Great Britain's colonies in North America, other European nations also had colonies in the continent. Some of those foreign settlements helped shape the two-hundred-year history of British colonial America.

Spain was the first European nation to claim an American colony. In 1492 Christopher Columbus led a Spanish expedition across the Atlantic hoping to reach China. Instead he arrived in the islands of the Caribbean Sea. Just a few decades later, the Spanish conquistadors invaded Mexico. After overthrowing the Native American Aztec civilization, they established a colony called New Spain that eventually controlled all of Mexico, much of Central America, and part of the present-day United States. By the middle of the sixteenth century, Spain had added what is now Florida, Texas, New Mexico, Arizona, Utah, Nevada, and California to its territory. Most of the colonial subjects in Spanish America lived in Mexico. Farther north, however, a few settlements took root. Among the earliest were St. Augustine, Florida, founded in 1565, and Santa Fe, New Mexico, founded in 1609.

Except for Florida, the Spanish colonies in North America were far from the part of the continent that the British occupied, and the British colonists had little to do with them. The French colony in North America, however, was much closer at hand.

France sent ships to the mouth of the St. Lawrence River, which is today the border between eastern Canada and the United States. In 1603 the French made their first attempt to settle a colony there, and in 1608 they established a lasting settlement at Quebec. New France, as their North American territory was called, grew into a large region around the St. Lawrence and the Great Lakes. The colonists of New France rubbed shoulders with the people of the British colonies that soon dotted the Atlantic coast south of the St. Lawrence.

Britain's claim to territory in North America was almost as old as Spain's. In 1497, while Columbus was still planning his third voyage to the Caribbean for Spain, King Henry VII of England hired a navigator named John Cabot to explore the strange new lands that Columbus had reported in the western Atlantic. Cabot is believed to have landed somewhere on the east coast of North America, probably in Newfoundland, an island that is now part of Canada. The English felt that Cabot's voyage gave them a territorial claim. For many years, however, the only English visitors to the New World were fishermen who braved the stormy North Atlantic to reach the rich fishing grounds off Newfoundland and the coast to the south. Fishing vessels from Portugal and western France also came to those waters and sometimes landed to get fresh water or trade with the local Native American people.

England did not become officially interested in North America until the late sixteenth century. At that time navigators were looking for something that geographers called the Northwest Passage, a sea route that would lead northwest from the Atlantic Ocean to China. Obsessed with finding this nonexistent passage, England saw North America as an obstacle, something to sail through or around. During the 1570s and 1580s, English explorers such as Martin Frobisher and John Davis probed its northeastern coast, searching for the Northwest Passage. They did not find it, but they did learn more about America, and some English explorers and merchants started thinking about planting colonies in eastern North America. Colonization would have several advantages. First, settlers in the North American wilderness would have to buy cloth, iron tools, glass, and other goods from British merchants. Second, the colonists could supply useful raw materials such as timber and furs. Perhaps they would even find gold. Ever since Spain had looted the golden riches of Mexico, Europeans had dreamed of finding another such source of immense wealth in the New World.

John White, one of the first Englishmen to try colonizing North America, painted this watercolor image of Native Americans in 1585. Such scenes were of great interest to Europeans, who were intensely curious about the land and people of the Americas.

Several groups of English merchants and investors tried to start colonies in North America in the late sixteenth and early seventeenth centuries. The 1580s saw the founding of a small colony on Roanoke Island off the coast of North Carolina. By 1590, however, the colony had disappeared. The fate of the Roanoke colonists remains a mystery. An early attempt to start a colony in Maine also failed. But in 1607 the English managed to establish a permanent settlement called Jamestown in Virginia. Thirteen years later the *Mayflower* brought the first settlers to New England—the name we still give to the northern part of the region that the English colonized.

Two other European nations founded settlements in eastern North America. The Dutch were building a far-flung empire of trade and colonization in Asia, but they also took an interest in North America, chiefly as a source of furs. In 1614 merchants from the Netherlands set up a trading post near present-day Albany, New York. Ten years later settlers began arriving in the colony that the Dutch called New Netherland, which stretched along the Hudson River. Its main town, New Amsterdam on Manhattan Island, had an excellent harbor and soon became a busy port. In 1638 Sweden established a small colony south of New Netherland on the Delaware River. It survived until 1655, when the Dutch captured it and added it to New Netherland. Nine years later the Dutch colony in turn fell to an English fleet sponsored by the Duke of York, and New Netherland became the English colony of New York.

By the middle of the eighteenth century, thirteen British colonies stretched along the Atlantic coast, from the border of New France in the north to the border of Spanish Florida in the south. (Britain also had colonies in the Caribbean islands known as the West Indies, but their history is not closely linked with that of the mainland colonies that became the United States.) More than a million and a half people lived in the thirteen colonies in 1760. Although this population included men and women from many national and ethnic backgrounds, most of the white colonists were from England, Scotland, Ireland, Germany, and the Netherlands. The overwhelming majority of blacks in colonial America were of West African heritage.

Although an ocean separated the North American colonies

from their parent countries, events in Europe had a powerful impact on colonial life. Conflicts in Europe spilled over into the colonies. When Great Britain and Spain went to war in the early eighteenth century, for example, fighting broke out between the Spanish in Florida and the southernmost British settlements. But the chief combatants of the colonial period were Britain and France, frequently at war in Europe and in the colonies.

The British and French colonies developed very differently. The British colonies had many more settlers and developed an agricultural economy in addition to exporting raw materials. Despite its large size, New France attracted far fewer settlers, and its economy was based almost entirely on trade, mostly in furs. Explorers, trappers, and traders from New France ranged far inland into the heart of the continent, while the British were slow to venture beyond the Appalachian Mountains, the western border of their colonies. The French colonists also forged closer ties than the British with the Native American peoples. While the British concentrated on developing their coastal colonies, the French built a network of forts, trading posts, and Indian alliances throughout the Great Lakes region, in the Ohio River valley, and along the Mississippi River. Eventually the British colonies were almost encircled by French-claimed territory.

Fighting between the French and the British broke out in the colonies when British colonists began buying furs and building forts on their northern and western frontiers—and sometimes beyond those frontiers. And when France and Great Britain went to war in Europe, their colonists also took up arms. The colonial period saw a series of such conflicts, ending in a prolonged war

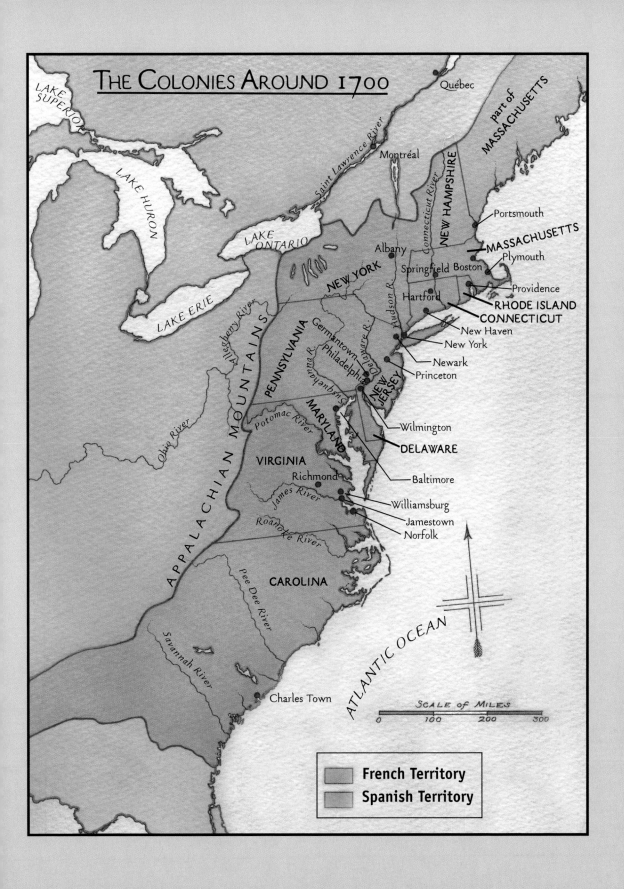

THE COLONIES AROUND 1700

LAKE SUPERIOR

LAKE HURON

LAKE ONTARIO

LAKE ERIE

Québec

Montréal

Saint Lawrence River

part of MASSACHUSETTS

NEW HAMPSHIRE

Connecticut River

Portsmouth

Albany

Springfield Boston

MASSACHUSETTS

Plymouth

NEW YORK

Hartford

Providence

RHODE ISLAND

CONNECTICUT

Hudson R.

New Haven

New York

Allegheny River

PENNSYLVANIA

Germantown

Philadelphia

Delaware R.

Newark

Princeton

APPALACHIAN MOUNTAINS

Susquehanna R.

NEW JERSEY

Wilmington

Ohio River

MARYLAND

Potomac River

DELAWARE

Baltimore

VIRGINIA

Richmond

James River

Williamsburg

Jamestown

Roanoke River

Norfolk

CAROLINA

Pee Dee River

Savannah River

ATLANTIC OCEAN

Charles Town

SCALE of MILES

0   100   200   300

French Territory

Spanish Territory

A picture from 1738 shows Canadian Indians using European firearms to hunt beaver for the fur trade.

between 1756 and 1763. In European history this war is known as the Seven Years' War, but the British colonists called it the French and Indian War because it pitted them against the French and their Indian allies. (These were more numerous and powerful than the Indians who sided with the British.) Fought largely on the frontier and in the Ohio River valley, the war ended in crushing defeat for New France when British forces captured Quebec and Montreal, the colony's two cities. The Treaty of Paris, which ended the conflict, gave France's territory in Canada and east of the Mississippi River to Great Britain.

Great Britain now controlled North America all the way to the Mississippi. British colonists were ready to stream across the Appalachians into the new territory, but Great Britain passed a law, called the Proclamation of 1763, that declared that the western limit of settlement was the summit of the Appalachians. The lands beyond were supposed to remain Indian territory, at least for a time. In this way, the British government hoped to avoid further fighting with the Native Americans and also to keep the colonists in the coastal settlements where they would be easier to govern and tax.

The Proclamation of 1763 enraged colonists who had thought they were fighting for access to the Ohio River valley. Some of them simply ignored the law and pushed westward over the mountains. But the proclamation was just one source of the frustration that many colonists felt with British rule by the middle of the eighteenth century. Conflicts over taxation and a growing desire for a voice in their own government drove the colonists ever closer to a break with Great Britain. In the mid-1770s their discontent boiled over into an armed rebellion that became the American Revolution and ended the colonial era.

In the pages that follow, you will find the words of dozens of people who lived in the American colonies. You will share the challenges of settling a new world, the experiences of daily life three centuries ago, and the turmoil of the unsettled years leading to rebellion. These are among the earliest American voices.

Jamestown, the first permanent English settlement in North America, began in 1607 as a small fort on the James River at the southern edge of Chesapeake Bay.

Chapter I

The Colonies Are Born

THE THIRTEEN BRITISH COLONIES WERE founded over a 125-year period with the permission of the crown, which formally controlled Britain's New World territory. The first was Virginia, which began with the settling of Jamestown in 1607. Its founders, the Virginia Company of London, obtained a charter from King James I allowing them to establish the colony. They hoped that Virginia would yield gold or other valuable goods (the most profitable item to come from the colony would be tobacco). In 1622 the desire for profitable trade—this time in fish and furs—led British investors to obtain a charter for the territory that eventually became New Hampshire and Maine, but they managed only to set up a few small outposts there.

Religious differences led to the founding of several settlements. Some members of the official church of England, the Anglican Church, believed that the church needed to be reformed or purified. They were called Puritans. Others, called Separatists, wanted to break away completely. The Separatists found religious freedom in the Netherlands but wanted to live in an English setting. The Virginia

Company agreed to let some of them settle in Virginia. Those who went to North America called themselves Pilgrims because they viewed the voyage as a pilgrimage, a journey with a religious or spiritual purpose. In 1620 a group of them sailed on the *Mayflower* and established the Plymouth colony outside the Virginia Company's charter. Ten years later a group of Puritans with a royal charter established the Massachusetts Bay Colony near Plymouth. Massachusetts grew in population and influence. It absorbed Maine, which never existed as a separate colony during the colonial period, and in 1691 it absorbed Plymouth. New Hampshire became a separate colony in 1679.

Lord Baltimore, a Catholic nobleman, established Maryland in 1632 as a refuge for Catholics, who were persecuted in England, where the majority of people were Protestants. Four years later colonists from Massachusetts formed two more colonies in New England.

Settlers dissatisfied with the Puritan leaders migrated to Connecticut and established their own government. Rhode Island was founded by people driven out of Massachusetts because of their religious beliefs, which had come to differ from Puritan ideas.

General James Edward Oglethorpe, founder of the Georgia colony. In England, Oglethorpe had headed a committee to study British prisons, where people were commonly imprisoned for debt. He hoped that in Georgia these debtors could settle down and become free, independent farmers.

In 1663 a group of noblemen acquired permission to establish the Carolina colony, hoping to make money from trade and land sales. (The colony would split into North and South Carolina in 1729.) The year after the founding of Carolina, the Duke of York acquired the Dutch and Swedish holdings along the Hudson and Delaware Rivers. He renamed the territory New York and gave its southern part to two friends, who founded New Jersey there. The last colony to be founded in what came to be called the Middle Atlantic region was Pennsylvania, created by a royal charter in 1681. The last of the thirteen colonies to be founded was also the southernmost. General James Oglethorpe founded Georgia in 1732; the colony served as a buffer between the British colonies and Spanish Florida and also offered an alternative to prison for people in debt.

John Smith Remembers Jamestown

One member of the expedition to establish a colony in Virginia was a twenty-seven-year-old soldier and adventurer named John Smith. Because Smith was at odds with the group's leader, or president, he had little voice in the colony at first. But after the ships that had brought the colonists returned to England and supplies ran low, the efficient and practical Smith helped guide the miserable and quarrelsome men of Jamestown through a period of hardship that survivors later called the "starving time." The colonists made Smith their governor from September 1608 to September 1609. Then, hounded by complaints and criticism, he returned to England. In 1624 he published *The Generall Historie of Virginia, New England, and the Summer Isles,* a description of British exploration and settlement in the Americas. It contained the following account, written by Smith and three other colonists, of events in Jamestown after the ships departed in June of 1607, leaving about one hundred men behind in the raw new colony.

BEING THUS LEFT TO OUR FORTUNES, it fortuned that within ten days scarce ten amongst us could either go, or well stand, such extreme weakness and sickness oppressed us. And thereat none need marvel, if they consider the cause and reason, which was this.

> "But now was all our provision spent . . . all helps abandoned . . . when God . . . so changed the hearts of the savages, that they brought such plenty of their fruits . . . as no man wanted."

Whilst the ships stayed, our allowance was somewhat bettered, by a daily proportion of biscuit, which the sailors would pilfer to sell, give, or exchange with us, for money, sassafras, furs, or love. But when they departed, there remained neither tavern, beer house, nor place of relief, but the common kettle. . . . [Our President kept the best food and allowed us] half a pint of wheat, and as much barley boiled with water for a man a day, and this having fried some 26 weeks in the ship's hold, contained as many worms as grains; so that we might truly call it rather so much bran than corn, our drink was water, our lodging castles in the air.

With this lodging and diet, our extreme toil in bearing and planting palisdades, so strained and bruised us, and our continual labor in the extremity of the heat had so weakened us, as were cause sufficient to have made us as miserable in our native country, or any other place in the world.

From May, to September, those that escaped, lived upon sturgeon, and sea crabs, fifty in this time we buried, the rest seeing the President's projects to escape these miseries in our pinnace by flight (who all this time had felt neither want nor sickness) so moved our dead spirits, as we deposed him. . . .

But now was all our provision spent, the sturgeon gone, all helps abandoned, each hour expecting the fury of the savages; when God the patron of all good endeavours, in that desperate extremity so changed the hearts of the savages, that they brought such plenty of their fruits, and provision, as no man wanted.

—Reprinted in John Lankford, editor, Captain John Smith's America. New York: Harper & Row, 1967.

THINK ABOUT THIS

1. What was the president of the colony planning to do before the settlers deposed him?
2. How would you describe the planning and leadership of the Jamestown colony in this first year?
3. Who saved the remaining men at Jamestown?

The Mayflower Compact: Settlers Define Their Rights

The Pilgrims who sailed to North America in 1620 planned to settle north of Jamestown in Virginia but landed much farther north, near Cape Cod in what became Massachusetts. They went ashore at a place called Plymouth, mapped six years earlier by Captain John Smith of Jamestown. The *Mayflower* passengers were not a tightly unified group with shared beliefs—of the one hundred and two people aboard, only forty were Pilgrims. The rest, called "strangers" by the Pilgrims, were craftspeople, laborers, and farmers that the Pilgrims had recruited in England to help them settle their

Modern paintings such as Clyde O. DeLand's *The Beginning of New England* show earnest, hardworking Pilgrims carving communities out of the wilderness. Although these images are not primary sources, they have become part of the shared American heritage.

colony. Knowing that they would need a way to govern this mixed community, the Pilgrim leaders wrote a compact, or agreement, under which they promised to make laws as needed and to obey them. All the men, Pilgrims and strangers alike, signed it. This document is called the Mayflower Compact. It is neither a system of government nor a constitution, but it sets forth the revolutionary idea that settlers in the new continent had a right and a responsibility to govern themselves.

In the Name of God, Amen. We whose names are underwritten, the loyal subjects of our dread Sovereign Lord King James, by the Grace of God of Great Britain, France and Ireland, King, Defender of the Faith, etc.

Having undertaken, for the Glory of God and our advancement of the Christian Faith and Honour of our King and Country, a Voyage to plant the First Colony in the Northern Parts of Virginia, do by these presents solemnly and mutually in the presence of God and one another, Covenant and Combine ourselves together into a Civil Body Politic, for our better ordering and preservation and furtherance of the ends aforesaid; and by virtue hereof to enact, constitute and frame such just and equal Laws, Ordinances, Acts, Constitutions and Offices, from time to time, as shall be thought most meet and convenient for the general good of the Colony, unto which we promise with all due submission and obedience. In witness whereof we have hereunder subscribed our names at Cape Cod, the 11th of November, in the year of the reign of our Soveriegn Lord King James, of England, France and Ireland the eighteenth, and of Scotland the fifty-fourth. Anno Domini 1620.

presents
the present words or statements

—*Quoted in Frank R. Donovan,* The Mayflower Compact. *New York: Grosset and Dunlap, 1968.*

THINK ABOUT THIS

1. What did the Pilgrims give as their reasons for coming to North America?
2. According to the compact, what characteristics would the Pilgrims' laws have?

William Penn Conducts a "Holy Experiment"

In 1682 King Charles II of England granted a huge tract of land in North America to William Penn in payment of a debt Charles had owed to Penn's father. (The king named the grant Pennsylvania, which means "Penn's woods" in Latin in honor of the senior Penn.) William Penn was a Quaker, a member of a Christian religious

This portrait of William Penn was made during Penn's lifetime and may be a reliable guide to his appearance. Later painters based their images of Penn on this drawing.

minority that had been persecuted in the British Isles. He declared that his colony would be a "Holy Experiment," a community shaped by the Quaker ideals of peace, equality, and tolerance, open to Christians of all sects. But Pennsylvania was more than an experiment in the Quaker way.

As proprietor, or owner, of the colony, William Penn expected to make money from the rents and taxes its people would pay. He advertised Pennsylvania's virtues and worked hard to attract settlers from several European countries. Penn also hoped that the thousand or so Europeans who were already living in Pennsylvania when he acquired it would stay there. In April 1681, before he arrived in his colony, he sent its residents this letter to introduce himself.

MY FRIENDS,

I wish you all happiness here and hereafter. These [words] are to let you know that it hath pleased God, in his providence, to cast you within my lot and care. It is a business that, though I never undertook before, yet God hath given me an understanding of my duty, and an honest mind to do it uprightly. I hope you will not be troubled at your change, and the King's choice, for you are now fixed at the mercy of no governor that comes to make his fortune great; you shall be governed by laws of your own making, and live a free, and if you will, a sober and industrious people. I shall not usurp the right of any, or oppress his person. God has furnished me with a better resolution, and has given me His grace to keep it. In short, whatever sober and free men can reasonably desire, for the security and improvement of their own happiness, I shall heartily comply with, and in five months resolve, if it please God, to see you. In the mean time, pray submit to the commands of my deputy, so far as they are consistent with the law, and pay him those dues (that formerly you paid to the order of the Governor of New York) for my use and benefit; and so I wish God to direct you in the way of righteousness, and therein prosper you and your children after you.

I am your true friend,

Wm. Penn

—*Quoted in Bonamy Dobrèe,* William Penn: Quaker and Pioneer.
Boston: Houghton Mifflin, 1932.

THINK ABOUT THIS

1. What advantages did Penn believe his proprietorship would offer to the residents of Pennsylvania?
2. What virtues or qualities did he encourage?
3. How would Penn's colony differ from what settlers had experienced in their homelands?

The Costs of Building a Colony: A Bill to the King

James Oglethorpe, founder of Georgia, asked the British government to repay money he had spent in Georgia "for the Preservation and Defence of His Majesty's Dominions on the Continent of North America." In 1743 Oglethorpe produced a list of hundreds of expenses, including those shown here. These are not dry accounting figures. Instead, they paint a lively picture of life in early Georgia, where the everyday business of mending wheelbarrows,

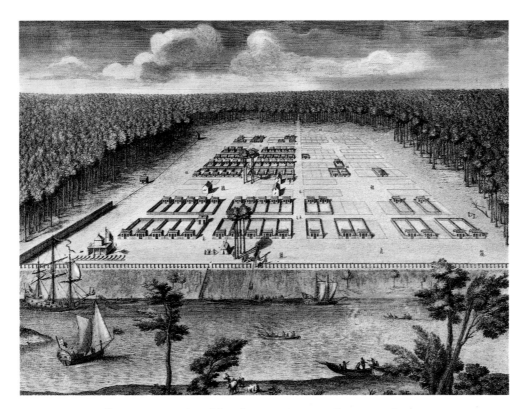

An engraving from 1734 is the oldest known image of Savannah, Georgia. By carefully comparing such artworks with written primary sources, historians can sometimes identify individual buildings.

patrolling borders, and trading with the Indians was enlivened by fires, arrests, and alligator hunts. The symbols at the top right of the list stand for pounds, shillings, and pence, the units of British currency at the time.

	£	S.	D.
To Captain Hugh Mackay for 10 boatchains,			
Padlocks, Staples and 45 feet of Chain.	5	4	0
To Edward Rush for mending and cleaning			
67 Indian guns.	1	2	6

To 5 Soldiers for assisting to put out a fire. 0   10   0

To Samuel Williams for killing an Allegator. 0   5   0

To Thomas Hucks Esqr and William West for
    15 Tons of Strong Beer in 8 Barrels with
    2 Iron Hoops each 119   8   0

To Thomas Marriott for Pipes and Tobacco for
    the Indians 0   2   0

To Francis Moore which he paid over to Sergeants
    Cook and Bailey and some others and to 7 Soldiers
    being a Gift to them on St. George's Day 2   7   6

To Michael Martin for taking a Deserter [capturing
    a runaway soldier]. 5   0   0

To Mary Matthews for her being Interpreter to the
    Chiefs of the Creek Indians 20   0   0

For sundry utensils for John Saller's Scout Boat 4   17   1½

For 7 pounds of meats and 7 pounds of bread
    each week for each of 100 privates, Highland
    Independent Company, 2 May 1740 to 2 September
    following 761   10   0

To Thomas Walker in full for a Roof to the Arsenal. 10   0   0

To Thomas Loop for mending Wheelbarrows 0   6   0

To John Brownfield for making 27 Shirts for Indians 1   13   9

—*Quoted in Webb Garrison,* Oglethorpe's Folly: The Birth of Georgia.
Lakemont, GA: Copple House Books, 1982.

THINK ABOUT THIS

1. Why do you think Oglethorpe paid for shirts, pipes, and other gifts for the Indians?

2. Why did Oglethorpe expect the British government to repay his expenses for arming and feeding soldiers?

Published in 1570 by Dutch mapmaker Abraham Ortelius, this map is titled "A New Description of America, or the New World." Less than a century after Columbus's first voyage, Europeans had explored most of the American coastline. The continents' interiors remained largely unknown, and mapmakers filled them with as much guesswork, rumor, and imagination as fact.

Chapter 2

A New World

CHRISTOPHER COLUMBUS AND JOHN CABOT believed that by sailing west across the Atlantic Ocean they had reached the eastern shore of China, whose fabled riches were the goal of European princes and merchants. They did not suspect that several large barriers lay between Europe and China—not only the Americas but also the immense Pacific Ocean.

Soon, however, European explorers and geographers realized that the lands on the far side of the Atlantic were unknown continents, and not part of Asia after all. In 1507 a German mapmaker named Martin Waldseemüller made a map of the world that showed a land mass west of Europe that was not connected to Asia. He labeled that land mass "America," in honor of an Italian navigator named Amerigo Vespucci, who had made several voyages across the Atlantic a few years earlier. Waldseemüller claimed that Vespucci's accounts of these voyages had added a "fourth part" to the world, after Europe, Asia, and Africa. Other mapmakers began using the name, and before long the new continents were known as the Americas.

They had another name as well: the New World, or *Mundus*

Novus as European scholars called it in Latin. Everything in this New World—the land, the native people and their civilizations, the plants and animals—was a surprise and a marvel to Europeans, to be described in detail and compared with familiar things from the known side of the ocean. But was the New World a paradise or a howling wilderness? From the earliest days of exploration to the end of the colonial period, people found it to be both. To some, North America seemed to be a lush garden, filled with abundant resources and natural marvels. Many felt that God had created it specially to be settled by Europeans—this belief certainly made it easier for the Europeans to overrun the Native Americans. Yet some people saw North America as dark and dangerous, populated by uncivilized savages and fierce beasts such as bears and wolves, by then quite rare in the settled parts of Europe. God may have wanted the Europeans to settle in North America, but doing so would be a test of faith that would require strength and courage. Sometimes the same place and the same circumstances awoke these very different responses in different people.

One challenge faced by everyone who explored or settled in North America was the complete absence, at least at first, of the comforts of home. The people who came to North America had to adjust to a new kind of life—harsher, perhaps, but for many it was more rewarding.

An Italian Explorer Meets the North Carolina Indians

Giovanni da Verrazano was one of the first Europeans to see the stretch of Atlantic coastline that later became the British colonies

This watercolor of a Carolina Algonquian man and woman was one of many painted by John White, an English artist and cartographer who accompanied Sir Walter Raleigh on his expedition to Virginia in 1585.

in North America. Hired by the king of France to look for a water passage from the Atlantic Ocean to China, Verrazano arrived in 1524 near Cape Fear in present-day North Carolina. He explored the coast all the way to Maine, and his account of the voyage was widely circulated in sixteenth-century Europe. It contains one of the first detailed descriptions of Native Americans to reach European readers.

THE PEOPLE ARE OF COLOR RUSSET and not much unlike Saracens; their hair black, thick, and not very long, which they tie together in a knot behind and wear it like a tail. They are well featured in their limbs, of mean stature, and commonly somewhat bigger than we. They are broad breasted, with strong arms. Their legs and other parts of the body are well fashioned and they are disfigured in nothing, saving that they have somewhat broad visages, and not all of them. For we saw many of them well favored, having great and black eyes, with a cheerful and steady look. They are not strong of body, yet sharp witted, nimble, and great runners. . . .

The people go entirely naked except that they cover their privy parts with certain skins of beasts like unto martens. They fasten these onto a narrow girdle made of grass, very artificially wrought, and

Saracen *old European term for the Muslim Arabs of the Middle East*

mean stature *average height*

visage *face*

artificially *artfully, cleverly*

hanged about with tails of divers [diverse] other beasts dangling about their bodies down to their knees. Some wear garlands of birds' feathers.

—*Quoted in Bill Lawrence,* The Early American Wilderness as the Explorers Saw It. *New York: Paragon House, 1991.*

THINK ABOUT THIS

Does Verrazano's description contain any clues about his opinion of the Indians he saw?

"A Hidious and Desolate Wildernes": A Pilgrim's Lament

Nearly a century after Verrazano's voyage, the *Mayflower* arrived at Cape Cod after a stormy and uncomfortable passage across the Atlantic. Pilgrim leader William Bradford, who was governor of Plymouth for many years, later wrote a history of its founding and early years. After being passed down within the Bradford family for generations, this manuscript was placed in a Boston church. During the American Revolution the British seized it and carried it off to London. Not until 1856 was Bradford's record discovered and published. It describes the Pilgrims' feelings when they first gazed upon the North American shore one November afternoon.

BEING THUS PASSED THE VAST OCEAN, and a sea of troubles before in their preparation . . . they had now no friends to wellcome them, nor inns to entertaine or refresh their weatherbeaten bodies, no houses or much less townes to repair too, to seek for succoure. . . . And for the season it was winter, and they that know the winters of that countrie know them to be sharp and violent, and subjecte to cruell and feirce stormes, deangerous to travill to known places, much more to serch an unknown coast. Besids, what could they see but a hidious and desolate wildernes, full of wild beasts and willd men? And what multituds ther might be of them they knew not. . . . [W]hich way soever

> "...they had now no friends to wellcome them, nor inns to entertaine or refresh their weatherbeaten bodys, no houses or much less townes to repair too."

they turnd their eys (save upward to the heavens) they could have little solace or content in respecte of any outward objects. For summer being done, all things stand upon them with a wetherbeaten face; and the whole countrie, full of woods and thickets, represented a wild and savage hiew. If they looked behind them, ther was the mighty ocean which they had passed, and was now as a maine barr and goulfe to separate them from all the civill parts of the world. . . . What could now sustaine them but the spirite of God and his grace? May not and ought not the children of these fathers rightly say: *Our fathers were Englishmen which came over this great ocean, and were ready to perish in this wildernes, but they cried unto the Lord, and he heard their voyce, and looked on their adversitie, etc.*

hiew (hue)
appearance

civill
civilized

—*Reprinted in William T. Davis, editor,* Bradford's History of Plymouth Plantation. *New York: Scribner, 1908.*

THINK ABOUT THIS

1. How would you describe Bradford's overall reaction to his first glimpse of the New World? Why do you think he felt that way?

2. As the Pilgrims faced the New World, what did Bradford see as their great support?

The Best Land in the World: A Pilgrim's Praise

In 1652 Mohawk Indians kidnapped sixteen-year-old Pierre Esprit Radisson from one of the French settlements in what is now Canada. Radisson spent several years traveling through upper New York and the Great Lakes region with the Mohawk before returning to the French colony. Soon he set off on a series of adventures beyond the settled frontier: in western New York, Michigan, Minnesota, and eventually Canada. In the 1660s Radisson went to work for the British. He helped them establish the Hudson's Bay fur-trading company and spent the final years of his life in England, where he wrote a chronicle of his adventures. Here he describes buffalo, which were unknown to Europeans but were once numerous around the Great Lakes. He then sums up his impressions of the North American landscape, which are very different from William Bradford's gloomy musings about the Massachusetts wilderness.

French explorer Louis Hennepin's *A New Discovery of a Vast Country in America* (1699) featured this illustration of a buffalo, one of many American animals completely unknown to Europeans.

The buff is a furious animal. . . . The horns of buffs are as those of an ox, but not so long, but bigger and of a blackish color. . . . He is reddish, his hair frizzled and very fine, all parts of his body much unto an ox. The biggest are bigger than any ox whatsoever. . . . It's a pleasure to find the place of their abode, for they turn round about, compassing two or three acres of land, beating the snow with the feet and, coming to the center, they lie down and rise again to eat the boughs of trees that they can reach. They go not out of the circle that they have made until hunger compels them.

> *"I can say that in my lifetime I never saw a more incomparable country."*

. . . The further we sojourned the delightfuller the land was to us. I can say that in my lifetime I never saw a more incomparable country. . . . The country was so pleasant, so beautiful and fruitful that it grieved me to see the world could not discover such enticing countries to live in. This I say because the Europeans fight for a rock in the sea against each other, or for a sterile and horrid country. Contrariwise, these kingdoms are so delicious and under so temperate a climate, plentiful of all things, the earth bringing forth its fruit twice a year, the people live long and lusty and wise in their way.

—*Quoted in Arthur T. Adams,* The Explorations of Pierre Esprit Radisson. *Minneapolis, MN: Ross and Haines, 1961.*

THINK ABOUT THIS

1. Why do you think Radisson considered it a "pleasure" to find the buffalos' resting places?
2. To what might Radisson have been referring when he speaks of Europeans fighting over rocks in the sea and "sterile and horrid" countries?

Daniel Boone fought Indians and founded settlements in Kentucky, in spite of the fact that settlement was officially forbidden there. Some later Americans came to see Boone as the ideal symbol of the frontier spirit.

Life without Bread: A Pioneer Diary

Great Britain tried to keep the colonists from crossing the Appalachian Mountains to settle in the Ohio River valley, which was supposed to remain in Indian hands. The colonists, however, kept pushing the frontier of settlement westward. Many crossed the mountains illegally to settle in the forbidden territory. Among them was Daniel Boone, who in March of 1775 led a group of pioneers into "Caintuck" (Kentucky). They built a fort on the Kentucky River and founded a settlement. William Call kept a diary of his family's arrival there. Here he describes how the pioneers laid out plots of land for their homesteads and the lottery system they used to determine which piece of land each family got. The last entry in the diary was written after the Calls ran out of flour. They would have no bread until the crops they planted produced grain the following year. Like the first settlers in America, the Kentucky pioneers soon used up what they had brought with them from home and had to live off the land.

THURSDAY 20TH—this morning is clear and cool. We start early and git Down to caintuck to Boons foart about 12 o'clock where we stop they come out to meet us and welcome us in with a voley of guns.

FRYDAY 21ST—warm this Day they begin laying out lots in the town and preparing for people to go to work to make corn.

SATTERDAY 22ND—they finish laying out lots this eavening I went a-fishing and caught 3 cats they meet in the night to draw for chois of lots but prefer it till morning.

cats
catfish

prefer
postpone

SUNDAY 23RD—this morning the peopel meets and draws for chois of lots this is a very warm day.

MONDAY 24TH—We all view our lots and some Don't like them about 12 o'clock the combses come to town and Next morning they make them a bark canew and set off down the river to meet their Companey.

" . . . this day we begin to live without bread."

TUESDAY 25TH—in the eavening we git us a plaise at the mouth of the creek and begin clearing.

WEDNESDAY 26TH—We Begin Building us a house and a plaise of Defense to Keep the indians off this day we begin to live without bread.

—*Quoted in Thomas Speed,* The Wilderness Road.
New York: Lenox Hill, 1971. Originally published in 1886.

THINK ABOUT THIS

1. Does the procedure for giving building lots to families sound fair to you?

2. How did the settlers react to the lottery system?

An Algonquian Indian village in North Carolina, painted by John
White around 1585. Such drawings are the closest things historians have
to primary-source images of traditional Native American life.

Chapter 3

The Native Americans

IN THE FIFTEENTH CENTURY, when the Europeans arrived, about four and a half million Native Americans lived in North America. Their ancestors had come to America from northeastern Asia many thousands of years before. Scientists are still not sure exactly when these first people reached the Americas, but it was certainly no later than 11,000 years ago, and possibly earlier.

They came during a long ice age, when great sheets of ice covered much of the northern world. Much of the earth's water was locked up in ice, and the seas were considerably lower than they are today. The belt of ocean that now separates Northeastern Asia and Alaska did not exist. Instead, the two land masses were connected by a strip of land that scientists call the Bering Land Bridge. Animals and people migrated across this bridge, and they and their descendants spread out and populated the Americas.

Over the centuries, the people of North America formed hundreds of distinct societies, each with its own language. Their ways of life varied. Some hunted walrus amid the ice and snow of the Arctic. Some dwelt in log houses in the eastern woodlands and combined hunting for deer and gardening edible plants. Others lived in many-roomed brick structures in the hot, dry Southwest and survived by using irrigation to water their fields of corn, beans, and squash. Despite this great variety, all of the native North American peoples had one thing in common: their world would change dramatically and forever with the coming of the Europeans.

First meetings between Native Americans and white Europeans took many forms and often involved misunderstandings on both sides. Columbus, for example, called the Native American people of the Caribbean "Indians" because he mistakenly thought that they were natives of India. The name stuck, although it was based on error. Similarly, the Aztec leader Montezuma thought that the Spanish adventurer Hernán Cortés was an embodiment of one of the Aztec gods, when in reality Cortés was an invader come to destroy Montezuma and his empire. Most first meetings, however, were far less dramatic. They were encounters between navigators or fishermen who had come ashore and local people who were curious about the pale-skinned strangers, their ships, and their strange possessions of steel and glass.

Many meetings ended in trade and the beginnings of communication. Friendships, or at least relationships based on mutual respect, did develop. Overall, however, the Europeans had a low opinion of people who were not Christian and whose culture was so different from their own. Their arrival was disastrous for the Indians. The Europeans killed some Native Americans with abuse or warfare, but many times more Indians died of diseases that were unknown in North America until the Europeans brought them. Europeans had long been used to smallpox and measles,

for example, but these illnesses wiped out whole communities and even societies of Native Americans. In the end, though, it was the Europeans' constant pressure to expand into North America, to take over land that had once belonged to the Indians, that created the greatest conflict between the two races.

Indians Provide Unexpected Aid to the Pilgrims

The Pilgrims worried much about the dangerous "savages" who "infested" North America. During their first few months at Plymouth, however, they caught only glimpses of Indians in the distance. In March of 1621 a Native American man walked into their midst. He has gone down in history as Samoset, originally from Maine. Samoset brought to Plymouth another Indian named Squanto, who was a great help to the colonists until his death in 1622, and a local chieftain named Massasoit, who made a treaty of peace with the colonists. Squanto not only spoke English but had

Another of White's watercolors. These pictures were in demand because Europeans were fascinated by details of the Indians' body paint, ornaments, and weapons, although they considered such things "savage."

been to England. An English adventurer had seized some Indians from the Massachusetts coast a few years earlier and sold them as slaves in Spain. Squanto was released and somehow got to England. He returned to Massachusetts on an exploring ship in 1619— only to find his people dead, probably killed by a European disease they had caught from explorers or fishermen. Squanto attached himself to the *Mayflower* colonists. This passage from Bradford's history of Plymouth describes the colonists' first meetings with the helpful Indians.

"Squanto . . . was a spetiall instrument sent of God for their good beyond their expectation. He . . . never left them till he dyed."

ALL THIS WHILE THE INDIANS CAME SKULKING about them, and would sometimes show them selves aloofe off, but when any approached near them, they would rune away. And once they stoale away their tools wher they had been at worke, and were gone to diner. But about the 16. of March a certaine Indian came bouldly amongst them, and spoke to them in broken English, which they could well understand, but marvelled at it. At length they understood by discourse with him, that he was not of these parts, but belonged to the eastrene parts, wher some English-ships came to fish, with whom he was acquainted, and could name sundrie of them by their names, amongst whom he had gott his language. He became profitable to them in acquainting them with many things concerning the state of the cuntry in the east-parts wher he lived, which was afterwards profitable unto them; as also of the people hear, of their names, number, and strength; of their situation and distance from this place, and who was cheefe amongst them. His name was Samaset; he tould them also of another Indian whos name was Squanto, a native of this place, who had been in England and could

speake better English than him selfe. Being, after some time of enter-
tainmente and gifts, dismist, a while after he came againe, and 5.
more with him, and they brought again all the tooles that were stolen
away before, and made way for the coming of their great Sachem,
called Massasoyt; who, about 4. or 5. days after, came with the cheefe
of his friends and other attendance, with the aforesaid Squanto . . .
Squanto continued with them, and was their interpreter, and was a
spetiall instrument sent of God for their good beyond their expectation. He directed them how to set their corne, wher to take fish, and
to procure other comodities, and was also their pilott to bring them to
unknowne places for their profitt, and never left them till he dyed.

—*Reprinted in William T. Davis, editor,* Bradford's History of Plymouth Plantation.
New York: Scribner, 1908.

THINK ABOUT THIS

1. Bradford offered two explanations for the appearance of English-
speaking Indians at Plymouth. What are they?

2. In what ways did Samoset help the settlers?

Indian Raid: A Colonist's Recollection of Horror

King Philip's War was a conflict between settlers and Native Americans that raged in New England in the 1670s. In November of 1675
a thousand colonists attacked a camp of the Narragansett and Nip-
muck people in Rhode Island and set it afire. Puritan preacher
Increase Mather wrote that "men, women, and Children (no man
knoweth how many hundreds of them) were burnt to death," and
his son Cotton Mather, also a preacher, reported gleefully that the

Indians had been barbecued. Three months later a force of Nipmucks and Narragansetts attacked the settlement of Lancaster, Massachusetts. They took twenty-four captives, including Mary Rowlandson and three of her children. She was separated from her ten-year-old daughter and fourteen-year-old son; a younger daughter, wounded in the attack, soon died. Rowlandson spent nearly twelve weeks as a servant of her captors before they exchanged her for some trade goods. Soon the Indians also released her surviving children. Her account of her experience, *A True History of the Captivity and Restoration of Mrs. Mary Rowlandson,* was published in 1682 and contains this description of the raid in which she was captured.

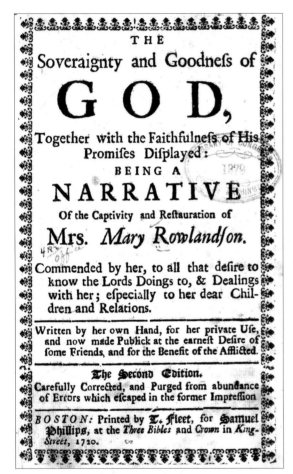

THE

Soveraignty and Goodnefs of

GOD,

Together with the Faithfulnefs of His Promifes Difplayed:

BEING A

NARRATIVE

Of the Captivity and Reftauration of

Mrs. *Mary Rowlandfon.*

Commended by her, to all that defire to know the Lords Doings to, & Dealings with her; efpecially to her dear Children and Relations.

Written by her own Hand, for her private Ufe, and now made Publick at the earneft Defire of fome Friends, and for the Benefit of the Afflicted.

The Second Edition.

Carefully Corrected, and Purged from abundance of Errors which efcaped in the former Impreffion

BOSTON: Printed by T. Fleet, for Samuel Phillips, at the *Three Bibles* and *Crown* in *King-Street,* 1720.

Mary Rowlandson's account of her 1675 capture in a Native American raid is one of many primary sources dealing with captivity among the Indians.

NOW IS THAT DREADFUL HOUR COME that I have often heard of. . . . Some in our House were fighting for their Lives, others wallowing in their Blood; the House on fire over our Heads, and the bloody Heathen ready to knock us on the Head if we stirred out. Now might we hear Mothers and Children crying out for themselves and one another, *Lord, what shall we do?* . . . But to return: the *Indians* laid hold of us, pulling me one way and the Children another, and said, *Come go along with us.* I told them they would kill me. They answered, *If I were willing to go along with them they would not hurt me*. . . . I had often before said, that if the *Indians* should come, I should chuse rather to be killed by them than taken alive; but when I came to the trial my mind changed; their glittering Weapons so daunted my Spirit, that I chose rather to go with those (as I may say) ravenous Bears, than that moment to end my daies. . . . Now away we must go with those Barbarous Creatures, with our bodies wounded and bleeding, and our hearts no less than our bodies.

—*Reprinted in William Andrews, editor,* Journeys in New Worlds: Early American Women's Narratives. *Madison, WI: University of Wisconsin Press, 1990.*

THINK ABOUT THIS

1. Why did Mary Rowlandson agree to go with the Indians?

2. Why do you think she wrote down her experience?

A Call for Help from the Frontier

In 1764, a year after the French and Indian War ended, the governor of Pennsylvania received a letter from Matthew Smith and James Gibson, two farmers on the colony's western frontier. The letter accused the governor of not giving citizens on the edge of the colony the same protections and privileges as those living closer to the capital of Philadelphia. Smith and Gibson wanted the frontier districts to be allowed to send more representatives to the House of Assembly, the colony's legislature. They were also vitally interested in issues of justice and punishment for Indians on the frontier, as this part of the letter shows.

DURING THE LATE AND PRESENT Indian wars, the frontiers of this Province
have been repeatedly attacked and ravaged by skulking parties of the
Indians, who have with the most savage cruelty murdered men, women,
and children without distinction, and have reduced near a thousand families to the most extream distress. It grieves us to the very heart to see
such of our frontier inhabitants as have escaped savage fury with the loss
of their parents, their children, their wives or relatives, left destitute by
the public, and exposed to the most cruel poverty and wretchedness
while upwards of an hundred and twenty of the savages who are with
great reason suspected of being guilty of these horrid barbarities under
the mask of friendship, have procured themselves to be taken under the
protection of government, with a view to elude the fury of the brave relatives of the murdered, and are now maintained at the public expense.

—*Reprinted in Samuel Eliot Morison,* Sources and Documents Illustrating the
American Revolution. *Oxford, England: Clarendon Press, 1923.*

THINK ABOUT THIS

1. What is the central complaint of this part of the letter?
2. How do you think the men who wrote the letter would like to deal with
the Indians who are under government protection?

Like Snow before the Sun: An Indian Chieftain Grieves for His People

The Native American peoples did not use written language in the
colonial period. Everything we know about them comes from the
writings of European explorers and colonists, and the words that

Indians are supposed to have spoken often sound very European when translated into English. A Cherokee leader named Dragging-Canoe is said to have made this speech to the council of his people in 1775, saying that they should not have sold their hunting lands to the whites. Even if the wording of the speech is not truly accurate, it reveals the pride and anger of Indians who saw their world being gobbled up by land-hungry outsiders.

"We will have our lands."

WHOLE NATIONS HAVE MELTED AWAY like balls of snow before the sun. The whites have passed the mountains and settled upon Cherokee lands, and now wish to have their usurpation sanctioned by the confirmation of a treaty. New cessions will be required, and the small remnant of my people will be compelled to seek a new retreat in some far distant wilderness. There they will be permitted to stay only a short while, until they again behold the advancing banners of the same greedy hosts. When the whites are unable to point out any farther retreat for the miserable Cherokees, they will proclaim the extinction of the whole race. Should we not therefore run all risks, and incur all consequences, rather than submit to further laceration of our territory? Such treaties may be all right for men too old to hunt or fight. As for me, I have my young warriors about me. We will have our lands.

—*Quoted in Robert L. Kinkaid,* The Wilderness Road. *New York: Bobbs-Merrill, 1947.*

THINK ABOUT THIS

1. What future did Dragging-Canoe foresee for his people? Do you think his vision of the future was correct?
2. What was the purpose of Dragging-Canoe's speech? What course of action did he wish to take?

Chapter 4

The First African Americans

EUROPEANS SOON LEARNED THAT the economies of some American colonies needed a lot of labor. Fur-trading did not call for large numbers of workers, but the kind of mining that the Spanish carried out in their Mexican and South American colonies did. So did plantation agriculture, the large-scale farming of crops for sale or export rather than for immediate use, which became the mainstay of the Caribbean colonies and the southern colonies of mainland British North America.

Slavery was one way that the organizers of colonies and the owners of plantations met their need for labor. Some attempted to harness the labor of captured Native Americans, but the extremely high death rate among the captives made this a poor solution. Early in the sixteenth century Spain began acquiring slaves on the coast of West Africa, usually by buying them from African slave merchants, and carrying them across the Atlantic to work in its Caribbean sugarcane plantations. The other European nations that had Caribbean colonies did the same, and soon African slavery was established in the islands and in the South American colonies of

Slave quarters aboard the Spanish slave ship *Albanoz* in 1846.
A British officer painted this watercolor after his ship captured the
Albanoz and freed the slaves. The British led the fight to end the slave
trade, but only after several centuries of importing slaves to their
colonies in the Caribbean and North America.

Spain and Portugal. In addition to Spanish slave traders, merchants from Portugal, the Netherlands, England, and France shipped loads of human cargo to these colonies.

It was not long before slavery gained a foothold north of the Caribbean as well. In 1619 a Dutch ship carrying the region's first Africans landed at a plantation on Chesapeake Bay, not far from Jamestown. It left about twenty Africans who were described as "servants," a term that at the time could mean either a hired servant or a slave.

By 1660, the Virginia colony's population included several hundred blacks, some of whom were free and owned property. One of these freemen, planter Anthony Johnson, had a black servant whom he claimed was "bound for life"—in other words, a slave. The growth of the Chesapeake colonies, with their large-scale agriculture, was accompanied by a steady growth in the slave trade and in the number of African-American slaves. By 1760 there were 285,000 blacks in the Chesapeake and Southern Colonies. Slavery was not limited to these regions, however; it existed in the North as well. There were almost 13,000 blacks in New England in

An eighteenth-century announcement of a slave sale. Using primary sources such as this, historians are working to document the scale and effects of the slave trade.

1760, and 29,000 in the Middle Atlantic colonies. While the great majority of the blacks were enslaved, some were free and supported themselves by operating businesses or practicing skilled trades such as blacksmithing and carpentry.

Not everyone approved of slavery; the Quakers, in particular, opposed it. As time went on, some colonists began to see that slavery was a violent and cruel institution and to believe that it was wrong. One of them was Thomas Jefferson, a plantation owner and slaveholder who became a leader in the British colonies' fight for independence. Jefferson was disturbed by slavery but did not know what to do about it—for example, he kept slaves and never freed them. For Jefferson, the thought of slavery was "like a fire-bell in the night," filling him with doubts and fears for the future.

A Slave in Virginia Writes to the Bishop of London

Many enslaved Africans in North America adopted the Christian religion. Some found comfort in it, and some found support for the idea that their enslavement was wrong. In 1723 the Church of England's bishop of London received a letter from a Virginia slave who would not sign his name, saying that he feared he might hang if his master heard of the matter. The writer, a Christian, compared the slaves in America to the biblical Children of Israel, the Jews, who were enslaved in Egypt in ancient times. He begged the bishop to do what he could to improve the condition of the slaves in the colonies.

HERE IT IS TO BE NOTED that one brother is a SLave to another and one Sister to an othe which is quite out of the way and as for mee my selfe I am my brothers SLave but my name is secrett . . . wee are commanded to keep holey the Sabbath day and we doo hardly know when it comes for our task mastrs are has hard with us as the Egypttions was with the Childdann of Issarall god be marcifll unto us

" . . . our task mastrs are has hard with us as the Egypttions was with the Childdann of Issarall."

here follows our Sevarity and Sorrowfull Sarvice we are hard used on Every account in the first place wee are in Ignorance of our Salvation and in the next place wee are kept out of the Church and matrimony is denied us and to be plain they doo Look no more upon us then if we ware dogs which I hope when these Strange Lines comes to your Lord Ships hands will be looket into. . . .

we desire that our Childarn be putt to Scool and Larnd to Reed through the Bybell which is all at prasant with our prayers to god for itts good Success before your honour these from your humbell Servants in the Lord my riting is

Known simply as *Head of a Negro*, this portrait is a study in dignity and humanity. It was made around 1777 by John Singleton Copley, a noted American-born painter who moved to England before the outbreak of the American Revolution.

vary bad I whope yr honour will take the will for the deede I am but a poore SLave that writ itt and has no other time butt Sunday and hardly that att Sumtimes

—*Quoted in Robin Blackburn,* The Making of New World Slavery.
London and New York: Verso, 1997.

THINK ABOUT THIS

1. What specific complaints does the writer of the letter outline to the bishop?
2. What improvements does he hope for?
3. How do you think he managed to send a letter to the bishop of London?

Two Slaveholders Voice Fears of Rebellion

The slaveholders of British America were keenly aware of their slaves' anger and resentment. Especially in the southern colonies, where the number of slaves was greatest and where their treatment was most severe, many whites feared an uprising. The two passages below, from letters written in the 1730s, show the concerns of two Virginians. The first was written by a colonial official, the second by a plantation owner and slaveholder named William Byrd.

[H]ERE THERE WAS A general rumour among [the slaves] that they were to be set free. And when they saw nothing came of it they grew angry and saucy, and met in the night-time in great numbers, and talked of rising; and in some places of choosing their leaders. But by patroulling; and whipping all that were found abroad at unseasonable hours, they quietly broke all this design, and in one County, where they had been discovered to talk of a general cutting off of their Masters, there were four of the Ring-leaders hanged.

We have already at least ten thousand men of these descendants of Ham fit to bear arms, and their numbers increase every day, as well by birth as by importation. And in case there should arise a man of desperate courage among us, exasperated by a desperate fortune, he might with more advantage than Cataline kindle a servile war. Such a man might be dreadfully mischievous before any opposition could be formed against him and tinge our rivers, wide as they are, with blood.

servile war
slave rebellion

—Quoted in Robin Blackburn, The Making of New World Slavery.
London and New York: Verso, 1997.

THINK ABOUT THIS

1. Do you think that the colonists' treatment of the "Ring-leaders," as described in the first letter, was justified?

2. What advice would you give to the writer of the second letter, and why?

Olaudah Equiano Tells How He Was Made a Slave

The vast majority of slaves in the New World did not have the tools to share their thoughts and experiences. Olaudah Equiano spoke for many. Equiano was born in West Africa around 1745. At age eleven he was seized by African slave traders and eventually loaded onto a slave ship. Equiano, whose first master gave him the name Gustavus Vassa, served ten years of enslavement in Pennsylvania and England. After obtaining his freedom from a Quaker master, he moved to England to work in the abolition movement, which strove to end slavery. In 1789 he published *Olaudah Equiano, or Gustavus Vassa, the African, Written by Himself.* These passages describe his capture and experiences on the ship.

ONE DAY, WHEN ALL OUR PEOPLE were gone out to their works as usual, and only I and my dear sister were left to mind the house, two men and a woman got over our walls, and in a moment seized us both, and without giving us time to cry out, or make resistance, they stopped our mouths, and ran off with us into the nearest wood. Here they tied our hands, and continued to carry us as far as they could, till night came on, when we reached a small house, where the robbers halted for refreshment, and spent the night. We were then unbound, but we unable to take any food; and, being quite overpowered by fatigue and grief, our only relief was sleep, which allayed our misfortune for a short time. . . . But alas! we were soon deprived of even the small comfort of weeping together. The next day proved a day of greater sorrow than I had yet experienced; for my sister and I were then separated, while we lay clasped in each other's arms.

. . . One day [the crew] had taken a number of fishes; and when they had killed and satisfied themselves with as many as they thought fit, to our astonishment who were on deck, rather than give any of them to us to eat, as we expected, they tossed the remaining fish into the sea again, although we begged and prayed for some as well as we could, but in vain; and some of my countrymen, being pressed by hunger, took an opportunity, when they thought no one saw them, of

Olaudah Equiano's firsthand account of capture and enslavement remains a useful primary source of information about the slave trade.

trying to get a little privately; but they were discovered, and the attempt procured them some very severe floggings. One day, when we had a smooth sea and moderate wind, two of my wearied countrymen who were chained together (I was near them at the time), preferring death to such a life of misery, somehow made through the nettings and jumped into the sea; immediately, another quite dejected fellow, who, on account of his illness, was suffered to be out of irons, also followed their example; and I believe many more would very soon have done the same, if they had not been prevented by the ship's crew, who were instantly alarmed. . . . [T]wo of the wretches were drowned, but they got the other, and afterwards flogged him unmercifully, for thus attempting to prefer death to slavery.

—*Reprinted in Arna Bontemps, editor,* Great Slave Narratives.
Boston: Beacon Press, 1969.

THINK ABOUT THIS

1. What do you think Equiano meant by "the nettings" on the ship?
2. How do you feel about the actions of the slaves who committed or attempted suicide?

Nobody to Look to but God: Old Elizabeth's Story

For many Africans in North America, one of the cruellest circumstances of slavery was being forced apart from their loved ones. Some endured the fate of Elizabeth, who was born to slave parents in Maryland in 1766. Elizabeth automatically became a slave, but she obtained her freedom when she was thirty. She lived to be a very old woman, and in the 1860s, during the Civil War, she published the story of her early years.

IN THE ELEVENTH YEAR OF MY AGE, my master sent me to another farm, several miles from my parents, brothers, and sisters, which was a great trouble to me. At last I grew so lonely and sad I thought I should die, if I did not see my mother. I asked the overseer if I might go, but being positively denied, I concluded to go without his knowledge. When I reached home my mother was away. I set off and walked twenty miles before I found her. I staid with her for several days, and we returned together. Next day I was sent back to my new place, which renewed my sorrow. At parting, my mother told me that I had "nobody in the wide world to look to but God." I went back repeating as I went, "none but God in the wide world." On reaching the farm, I found the overseer was displeased at me for going without his liberty. He tied me with a rope, and gave me some stripes [lashes] of which I carried the marks for weeks.

"At last I grew so lonely and sad I thought I should die, if I did not see my mother."

liberty
permission

—*Reprinted in Henry Louis Gates, editor,* Six Women's Slave Narratives.
New York: Oxford University Press, 1988.

THINK ABOUT THIS

1. What are some reasons why slaveholders might have separated slaves from their families?
2. What role do you think religion played in the lives of Elizabeth and her mother?

One of a settler's first tasks was to clear land for farming.
New fields were dotted with stumps. Removing the stumps was so
difficult that many colonists simply worked around them
when planting, weeding, and harvesting their crops.

Chapter 5

Daily Life

THE WORDS "COLONIAL AMERICA" call up certain time-honored images and ideas. They make us think of the groups of people who came to America with particular purposes, such as the gentlemen adventurers of Jamestown or the Puritans planning to create a new society. Captain John Smith, Pocahontas, William Penn, and other colorful, notable individuals come to mind. But historian John J. Waters has pointed out that as many as one-fifth of all the European immigrants who came to North America did so on their own, for private reasons, without any connection to the formal chartered groups and companies. Beyond the big names and the big events such as first landings and wars, colonial America was made up of thousands of ordinary people going about their everyday lives.

Most of them lived in the countryside. British North America was overwhelmingly rural and agricultural throughout the colonial period. Even in 1800, well after the colonial era ended, more than nine out of every ten people in the new United States lived in the country. The majority of them were farmers or laborers on farms owned by other people. Skilled workers who practiced their trades in the country, such as blacksmiths and carpenters, also generally owned land and farmed it. The typical colonial family lived in an isolated farmhouse. Family members made goods such as clothes and candles for themselves. They visited the marketplaces of the nearest village or town once a month or so. They went to church weekly or more often if they could, and if they couldn't they held family prayers and Bible readings.

But the image of the colonial village, complete with white steeple and tidy houses clustered around a central green, is not a myth. Such centers did form, especially in New England, where Puritan ideas about community life regulated settlement for a long time. There and in other parts of the colonies, some communities grew into towns and even cities. Almost from its beginning, New Amsterdam—later New York City—was a thriving urban center because of the activity at its port. Other ports also grew into major colonial cities. By the end of the colonial period, the two biggest cities were Philadelphia, with a population of 28,000, and New York, with 25,000 inhabitants.

Although the colonies were primarily agricultural, farming styles varied from place to place. The southern colonies practiced plantation agriculture, growing large amounts of crops such as tobacco, rice, and cotton to sell to merchants who exported these goods outside the colonies. The middle colonies also grew cash crops for sale, but they produced chiefly wheat. They also marketed livestock. In New England, where growing seasons were shorter and the soil was thinner and less fertile, people practiced subsistence farming, producing food crops for their own use.

By the middle of the eighteenth century, New York and Brooklyn were busy centers of commerce, linked by a regular ferry.

Throughout the colonies, daily life for most people centered on work. Only a small fraction of the total population was rich enough to be idle.

A Doctor in the House: Folk Remedies in the Colonies

Doctors were rare in colonial America, especially in the early years. When sickness struck, most people treated themselves and their families. They depended upon folk medicine, traditional remedies and cures passed down from generation to generation. The following folk remedies from the seventeenth century show how people treated common medical problems. The first one is about using the root of the sassafras tree as a health tonic, the second tells how to treat the swelling caused by toothache, and the third describes a treatment for styes, or swellings on the eyelids.

One of the most respected businessmen in a colonial town was the apothecary, who acted as both doctor and druggist and mixed medicines, salves, and even perfumes in his shop.

In the spring of the year,
When the blood is too thick,
There is nothing so rare
As the sassafras stick.
It cleans up the liver,
It strengthens the heart,
And to the whole system
New life doth impart.
Sassafras, oh, sassafras!
Thou art the stuff for me!
And in the spring I love to sing
Sweet sassafras! of thee.

• • •

They boil gruel of maize and milk; to this they add, whilst it is yet over the fire, some of the fat of hogs or other suet and stir it well, that everything mix equally. A handkerchief is then spread over the gruel and applied as hot as possible to the swelled cheek, where it is kept till it is gone cool again.

A small and pleasant craft of the blacksmith was to remove styes from the eyes of children. They were sent to him to ask him to do it, and he'd say, "Just wait till I've done this horseshoe," and the child would push close to watch, close to the heat and the steam, and blink hard, every time the great hammer came down with a bang—till in half an hour the smith would wipe his hands, and look, and smile (for the stye had burst and wept itself away).

—*Quoted in David Freeman Hawke,* Everyday Life in Colonial America. *New York: Harper and Row, 1988.*

THINK ABOUT THIS

1. Do you think that most households would have been able to use these methods? Would they have had the necessary ingredients or tools at hand?

2. Why do you think the author of the third account says removing styes is a "pleasant craft"?

Everyday Business: Buying Ribbon in a General Store

Sarah Kemble Knight lived in Boston. In 1704, at the age of thirty-eight, she set out to do something rather unusual for a woman in colonial America—to travel to another city alone on horseback. Knight's journey to New York took her through country villages, along bumpy and muddy roads, across streams, and into shabby country inns. All of it was a revelation to the well-bred city dweller, who arrived safely at her destination and wrote about her experiences. Here she describes a couple of "country folk" in a general store in New Haven, Connecticut. Knight calls the woman "Joan Tawdry," a sort of nickname for any woman of the lower classes (*tawdry* means "shabby" or "cheap").

IN COMES A TALL COUNTRY FELLOW, with his cheeks full of tobacco, for they seldom lose their cud but keep chewing and spitting as long as their eyes are open. He advanced to the middle of the room, makes an awkward nod, and spitting a large deal of aromatic tincture, he gave a scrape with his shovel-like shoe, leaving a small shovel full of dirt on the floor, made a full stop, hugging his own pretty body with his hands under his arms, stood staring around him, like a cat let out of a basket. At last, like the creature Balaam rode on, he opened his mouth and said:

> *"... they serve themselves well, making the merchants stay long enough for their pay."*

"Have you any ribbon for hatbands to sell, I pray?"

The questions and answers about the pay being past, the ribbon is brought out and opened. Bumpkin simpers, cries "it's confounded gay, I vow," and beckoning to the door, in comes Joan Tawdry, dropping about fifty curtesies and stands by him. He shows her the ribbon.

gent
short for genteel, meaning refined or elegant

"Law, you," says she, "it's gent. Do you take it, 'tis dreadfully pretty."

Then she inquires, "Have you any good silk, I pray?" which being brought and bought, "Have you any thread silk to sew it with?" says she, which being accommodated with they departed.

They generally stand after they come in a great while speechless, and don't say a word until they are asked what they want, which I impute to the awe they stand in of the merchants, who they are constantly almost indebted to, and must take what they bring without liberty to choose for themselves; but they serve themselves well, making the merchants stay long enough for their pay.

—Sarah Kemble Knight, Journal, *reprinted in Perry Miller and Thomas H. Johnson, editors,* The Puritans: A Source Book of Their Writings. *New Haven, CT: Yale University Press, 1963. Originally published in 1825.*

Think about This

What was Sarah Kemble Knight's attitude toward the people she describes?

Colonial Recreation: A Dramatic Bull Bait

Some colonial sports and entertainment seem cruel in modern eyes. Bull baiting, in which spectators watched dogs attack a bull, was one such sport. Imported from England, it was popular everywhere in America. A Philadelphia man wrote about a startling event at a bull bait in the middle of the eighteenth century, when notions such as the prevention of cruelty to animals and animal rights still lay far in the future.

THE ANIMAL WAS IN A GREAT RAGE, tho' much exhausted before I reached the scene of action. Soon after I got there, the bull threw a small mastiff about ten foot high, which he hooked in the upper jaw and tore it nearly off with every tooth in it. A new pack of dogs were now prepared for the combat, and every eye turned toward them.

At this moment who should break through the ring suddenly but the beautiful Polly Heffernan (for that was her name). She was beholding the battle through the cracks of the high fence which closed the field on South Street, and pitying the persecuted animal she scaled it unseen by the crowd, which she pierced like a dart, and run directly up to the bull, without shoes or stockings on, her bosom bare and her ringlets of beautiful black hair flowing in wild disorder upon her neck and shoulders. Her clothing was nothing but her long shift and a white petticoat, so that if ghosts are she appeared more like a ghost than a human being.

"Not a man dared to enter the ring to save her, but all stood trembling for Polly's life."

When she reached the bull, which almost immediately before was in a great rage, he dropped his ears and bowing his head as if he knew his deliverer was come, she thus accosted him:

"Poor bully! And have they hurt thee? They shall not hurt thee any more," and stroking his forehead she repeated, "They shall not hurt thee any more."

We multitude were confounded and dumbstruck with amazement. Not a man dared to enter the ring to save her, but all stood trembling for Polly's life. In the midst of their gaze, she darted back like an arrow from the bow, over the fence, and returned to the hospital from which she eloped and here the bait ended.

—*Quoted in David Freeman Hawke,* Everyday Life in Colonial America. *New York: Harper and Row, 1988.*

THINK ABOUT THIS

Why do you think the bait ended after Polly Heffernan's surprising appearance?

Country Life and Customs: A Minister's Journal

In 1775 and 1776, just as the Revolutionary War was beginning, a 28-year-old New Jersey man named Philip Vickers Fithian traveled through western Virginia, Maryland, and Pennsylvania as a missionary, spreading the word of the Presbyterian church and preaching in tiny towns that did not have ministers. Fithian's journal of the trip is a gentle, often humorous look at everyday life in the frontier settlements that colonial Americans called "the backcountry." In these passages Fithian describes a new settlement and foretells its future—today it is Martinsburg, West Virginia. He then gives a view of life in a nameless hamlet, or small village, tucked away in a western Pennsylvania valley.

MAY 19. MARTIN'SBURG

. . . This village derives its Name from Col: Martin, a Nephew of Lord Fairfax—It is yet in Infancy—Two Years ago the Spot was high Woods—There are now perhaps thirty Houses, they have already built a Prison of Stone & strong—And are now making a Courthouse of no inconsiderable Size and & Eligance—Probably, if American Liberty be established, for which we are now contending even in Blood, this, with many other infant Villages, in a Series of Years, will be populous & wealthy Towns, grand in Appearance, & busy with Commerce—Especially if the Navigation up this long River

"*. . . the Glory of America, her Wealth & Inhabitants, and inchanting Habitations, are remote yet, & to be obtained by Time, & Industry.*"

can be effected—But the Glory of America, her Wealth & Inhabitants, and inchanting Habitations, are remote yet, & to be obtained by Time, & Industry—

Expence to Day 0/0. Distance 15 Miles.

THURSDAY AUGUST 10

Cleanliness & Smartness are visible in our little Hamlet.—All is suitable but this going to Bed & rising in the same Room, & often in full view, of the whole Family—This, to be sure, puts me often to the Blush.

cymbalines
doughnuts

paste
porridge or gruel

carnage
meat

We have here no Meat of any kind. Our Breakfasts are Milk, with Bread & Butter; with these at Dinner we have the Addition of Cymbalines—And for Supper we have only Paste & Milk. It is a rich Repast we have with these original and natural Supports to Life, Health & Vivacity—I feel brisk & vigorous; & am, surely, growing fat, I fear corpulent, upon these natural Luxuries. *Simplicity* in Living, & Health—Much Carnage in Diet, & several Kinds at the same Time, & all highly, & differently seasoned; Great Quantity & Variety of strong Liquors, which grow poisonous by untimely & immoderate Application—These stop up & darken the Understanding, they effect that Languor & burdensome Dullness which makes Life & all her Duties appear to many tiresome beyond Measure.

Thompson who came over the Mountains with me is a Droll. Last Night our Fire was almost out.—"*Peggy,*" quoth he, "bring in some Bark to save the Fire"—"Indeed, Tom," answered the Girl, "I am tired, pulling Flax all Day, & cant."—"Well then," quo' Tom, "run out & call in the Neighbours to see it *die.*"

"I observe among the People here . . . the greatest Plainness & Familiarity in Conversation."

I observe among the People here, & Mr. Fleming tells me it is universal, the greatest Plainness & Familiarity in Conversation; every Man, in all Companies, with

All colonial girls, except the richest, learned to use a spinning wheel. They spun wool into yarn and spun flax, a plant fiber, into thread. They also learned to weave the yarn and thread into "homespun" cloth.

almost no Exception, Calls his Wife, Brother, Neighbour, or Acquaintance, by their proper Name of Sally, John, James, or Michael, without ever prefixing the customary Compliment, of "My Dear," Sir, Mr. &c.

—Reprinted in Robert G. Albion, editor, Philip Vickers Fithian: Journal, 1775–1776. *Princeton. NJ: Princeton University Press, 1934.*

THINK ABOUT THIS

1. Can you suggest reasons why the people of Martinsburg constructed a strong prison as their first public building?
2. How would you describe Fithian's attitude toward life in the country?
3. What did Fithian mean by "Plainness and Familiarity in Conversation"? Do you think he thought this was an admirable quality of the people he met?

An Indentured Servant Tells Her Story

A great number of the people who came to British America did so in some form of bondage. Some were slaves, but many others were servants bound by a system called indenture. Under this system, people who could not afford the high costs of moving to the New World agreed to work for a set period of time (usually two to seven years) for whoever paid their passage. Masters could sell or trade the labor contracts of these indentured servants, who had few rights under the law. Historian Philip Morgan estimates that as many as two-thirds of all white immigrants to the British American colonies were indentured servants. The system provided much-needed labor for the growing colonies and made it possible for many men and women to cross the Atlantic who could never have paid for the journey on their own. Yet the life of an indentured servant could be hard, as the story of Elizabeth Ashbridge reveals. A ship's captain offered her passage from Ireland to New York in 1732, but upon her arrival he made her sign an indenture to pay what she owed him. Later in life Ashbridge became a Quaker missionary, returned to Ireland, and wrote an account of her life. This passage begins with the captain's threats in New York.

"... Were it Possible to Convey ... a sense of the Sufferings of my Servitude, it would make the most strong heart pity the Misfortunes of a young creature as I was."

I THEREFORE IN A FRIGHT SIGNED [the indenture], & tho' there was no Magistrate present, I being Ignorant in such Cases, it Did well enough to Make me a Servant four Years.

In Two Weeks time I was Sold, & Were it Possible to Convey in Characters a sense of the Sufferings of my Servitude, it would make the most strong heart pity the Misfortunes of a young creature as I was, who had a Tender Education; for tho' my Father had no great Estate, yet he Lived well. I had been used to Little but my School, but now it had been better for me if I had been brought up to more hardship. For a While I was Pretty well used, but in a Little time the Scale turned, Occasioned by a Difference that happened between my Master & me, wherein I was Innocent: from that time he set himself against me and was Inhuman. He would not suffer me to have Clothes to be Decent in, having to go barefoot in his Service in the Snowey Weather & the Meanest Drudgery, wherein I suffered the Utmost Hardship that my Body was able to Bear, which, with the afforesaid Troubles, had like to have been my Ruin to all Eternity had not Almighty God in Mercy Interposed.

—Reprinted in William Andrews, editor, Journeys in New Worlds: Early American Women's Narratives. Madison, WI: University of Wisconsin Press, 1990.

THINK ABOUT THIS

Do you think the indenture system was fair? Why or why not?

Portrait of a colonial family: The husband and father wears a dark suit, his wife wears a cap, and their ten children range from infants to adults. Colonial families were large, and households were generally crowded.

Chapter 6

Childhood and Family Life

DURING THE COLONIAL PERIOD, people in the British Isles shared some basic ideas about family life. They carried these ideas with them to the New World and attempted to reproduce familiar family patterns there, although the new circumstances they met in North America caused some of their ideas and customs to change over time.

The British North American colonists shared the common belief that the nuclear family—a married couple and their children—was the most important unit of society. An individual's family determined his or her social status and was a large portion of his or her personal identity. Families were also economic units. Whether on farms or in stores or workshops, families, not companies, did most of the work in the colonies. Often, however, a family expanded into a household that included people other than the nuclear family. Elderly parents, relatives without households of their own, and servants often lived with families. Sometimes the line between servants and relatives was blurred. It was common for poor families to send a son or daughter to live with and work for a more prosperous relative.

Colonial family life rested on belief in the authority of men. Fathers and husbands had a high degree of control over their children and wives. A boy eventually grew up and acquired his own legal identity, but in most cases girls were considered dependents of their fathers until they married, at which time they became dependents of their husbands, with no separate legal identity. Married women could not own property, make wills, or sign contracts on their own. Women whose husbands had died, however, had considerable independence.

Colonists in British North America faced dangers they had not known in the British Isles. In some areas Indian wars were a hazard. In the Chesapeake Bay area and farther south, diseases such as malaria and typhus took a very high toll. Most families lost several children in infancy, and the high death rate meant that many young people were orphaned and grew up with relatives, family friends, or foster parents. Because so many men and women lost their spouses, remarriage was also common, and blended families of stepsiblings were normal. New England was the healthiest part of the colonies, and more families remained unbroken there than anywhere else.

Colonial families tended to be large, and households were generally crowded. Rare was the child who had a room or even a bed to himself or herself. Once children reached the age of seven or so, they had responsibilities. Girls cared for their younger siblings and helped their mothers with scores of tasks, from tending gardens to feeding chickens to spinning wool. Boys helped their fathers with planting and harvesting, tending livestock, or cutting firewood. By the time young people were teenagers, they were considered valuable sources of labor. Girls might earn money—or at least their room and board—by working for other families as servants. Boys might be apprenticed, or sent to work for a professional or crafts worker in exchange for training in a trade. Life was not all work, however. Events such as barn-buildings and town meetings gave young people a chance to enjoy one another's company. More daring pleasures, such as dancing and attending plays, were available in the cities.

Etiquette for Children: The School of Manners

Colonial Americans were greatly concerned with courtesy and manners. Rudeness was seen as a threat to the order and discipline of the whole community. Records of lawsuits show that people frequently went to court for such violations as name-calling and making faces. Parents took great pains to teach their children to act properly. Notions of good etiquette and manners were based on the customs of upper-class people, or gentlemen and gentlewomen. People at all levels of society wanted their children to copy the behavior of gentlefolk, and they turned to handbooks that outlined proper behavior for children. A handbook called *The School of Manners* was published in London in 1701 and became very popular with parents in the American colonies. Among its instructions to the young were the following mealtime rules.

Never sit down at the table till asked, and after the blessing.

Ask for nothing; tarry till it be offered thee.

Speak not.

Sing not, hum not, wriggle not.

Bite not thy bread but break it.

Take not salt with a greasy knife.

Dip not the meat in the same [the salt].

Look not earnestly at any other that is eating.

Spit not, cough not, nor blow thy nose at table if it may be avoided;
    but if there be necessity, do it aside, and without much notice.

Lean not thy elbow on the table, or on the back of thy chair.

Stuff not thy mouth so as to fill thy cheeks; be content with smaller
    mouthfuls.

Blow not thy meat, but with patience wait till it be cool.

Eat not too fast nor with greedy behavior.

Eat not vastly but moderately.

Make not noise with thy tongue, mouth, lips, or breath in thy eating
    and drinking.

Smell not of thy meat; nor put it to thy nose; turn it not to the
    other side upward on thy plate.

When moderately satisfied, leave the table.

—*Quoted in Alice Morse Earle,* Child Life in Colonial Days.
New York: Macmillan, 1899.

THINK ABOUT THIS

1. How do these rules of etiquette compare with the way people eat today?
2. What do the rules tell us about the kinds of food people ate and the way they ate it?

The Well-Dressed Colonial Boy and Girl: Two Family Accounts

Colonial boys and girls wore long smocks, called petticoats or coats, until they were about six years old. Under these they wore linen underclothing, and over them they wore woolen shawls or overshirts for warmth in cold weather. At about age six, children began wearing clothes that were miniature versions of adult garments. Boys wore tight-fitting pants called breeches or britches. Girls wore dresses. The following lists show the kinds of clothes worn by children of well-to-do gentlemen. Children from humbler families wore similar clothes, but theirs were made of coarser fabric, such as burlap or homespun linen or wool. The first list was made in the late 1600s. It shows the clothing ordered for a ten-year-old boy who was being sent away to school. The list mentions osenbrig, stuff, and serge, which are types of cloth. Cravats are ties, and a wastecoat, or waistcoat, is a vest. The second list dates from 1761. It was written by George Washington when he ordered clothes from London for his six-year-old stepdaughter. Lawn, cambrick, callimanco, and worsted are types of cloth. A frock is a dress, a capuchin is a long cloak with a hood, and egrettes or aigrettes are ornaments worn pinned to the hair or to hats.

"Eleven new shirts, 4 pair laced sleeves, 8 Plane cravats, 4 Cravats with Lace . . ."

ELEVEN NEW SHIRTS, 4 pair laced sleeves, 8 Plane cravats, 4 Cravats with Lace, 4 Stripte Wastecoats with black buttons, 1 Flowered Wastecoat, 4 New osenbrig Britches, 1 Gray hat with a black ribbon, 1 Gray hat with a blew ribbon, 1 Dousin black buttons, 1 Dousin coloured buttons, 3 Pair gold buttons, 3 Pair silver buttons, 2 Pair Fine blew Stockings, 1 Pair Fine red Stockings, 4 White Handkerchiefs, 2 Speckled Handkerchiefs, 5 Pair Gloves, 1 Stuff Coat with black buttons, 1 Cloth Coat, 1 Pair blew plush britches, 1 Pair Serge britches, 2 Combs, 1 Pair new Shooes, Silk & Thred to mend his Cloathes.

—*Shirley Glubok, editor,* Home and Child Life in Colonial Days. *New York: Macmillan, 1969.*

1 COAT MADE OF FASHIONABLE SILK. A Fashionable Cap or fillet with Bib apron. Ruffles and Tuckers, to be laced. 4 Fashionable Dresses made of Long Lawn. 2 Fine Cambrick Frocks. A Satin Capuchin, hat, and neckatees. A Persian Quilted Coat. 1 p. Pack Thread Stays. 4 p. Callimanco Shoes. 6 p. Leather Shoes. 2 p. Satin Shoes with flat ties. 6 p. Fine Cotton Stockings. 4 p. White Worsted Stockings. 12 p. Mitts. 6 p. White Kid Gloves. 1 p. Silver Shoe Buckles. 1 p. Neat Sleeve buttons. 6 Handsome Egrettes Different Sorts. 6 Yards Ribbon for Egrettes. 12 Yards Coarse Green Callimanco.

—*Quoted in Alice Morse Earle,* Child Life in Colonial Days. *New York: Macmillan, 1899.*

THINK ABOUT THIS

1. What are the differences between these wardrobes and the typical clothes of a boy or girl today?

2. How do your think your life would be different if you wore these clothes?

A Connecticut Youth's Education

Abraham Pierson was born in Killingworth, Connecticut, in 1756. When he grew up, he kept a journal in which he described his childhood, including his education. Young people in the colonies often had to help their parents work on their farms or in their stores or workshops. Like many children, Pierson did not go to school regularly. He managed to learn quite a lot, however, with the help of his parents. Colonial Americans regarded education as a family responsibility.

"While I was young I had but little opportunity of going to School having Sometimes not more than 5 or 6 weeks Schooling in a year."

WHILE I WAS YOUNG I had but little opportunity of going to School having Sometimes not more than 5 or 6 weeks Schooling in a year and at most not more than 10 weeks and many years there was no School at all but notwithstanding the little Schooling I had yet being instructed by my Parents I became able when about 7 years old to read tolerable well in a Bible So as that when I was 8 years old I had almost read the Bible through. I read once every morning Constantly when there was no School and began to learn to write and within a few years I made Some Progress in Arithmetic learn'd the Ground Rules and Several other Useful Rules.

—*Quoted in Jacob Ernest Cooke, editor,* Encyclopedia of the North American Colonies, Volume 2. *New York: Scribner's, 1993.*

1. What kinds of knowledge did Pierson acquire as a child?

2. How would you compare his education with that of a modern youngster?

Bad Deeds and Good Deeds: Mary Osgood Sumner's Journal

Now the Child being entred in his Letters and Spelling, let him learn thefe and fuch like Sentences by Heart, whereby he will be both inftructed in his Duty, and encouraged in his Learning.

The Dutiful Child's Promifes,

I Will fear GOD, and honour the KING.
I will honour my Father & Mother.
I will Obey my Superiours.
I will Submit to my Elders.
I will Love my Friends.
I will hate no Man.
I will forgive my Enemies, and pray to God for them.
I will as much as in me lies keep all God's Holy Commandments.

The New England Primer was designed to teach children not just reading skills but proper behavior as well.

In both England and Massachusetts, the Puritans had a tradition of questioning themselves about how they lived their lives. They wanted to "improve" their time, which meant doing useful or educational things. They also felt that it was important for each person to recognize what he or she had done wrong each day—this might prevent it from happening again. Many Puritans kept journals in which they wrote down the events of each day and their thoughts about them. A South Carolina girl named Mary Osgood Sumner was descended from Puritan ancestors from Dorchester, Massachusetts. She kept up the old habit of examining her daily life in a journal. On pages labeled "Black Leaf" she recorded her errors and faults. Those labeled "White Leaf" were for her duties and good deeds.

BLACK LEAF

JULY 8. I left my staise on the bed.

JULY 9. Misplaced Sister's sash.

JULY 10. Spoke in haste to my little Sister, spilt the cream on the floor in the closet.

JULY 12. I left Sister Cynthia's frock on the bed.

JULY 16. I left the brush on the chair; was not diligent in learning at school.

JULY 17. I left my fan on the bed.

JULY 19. I got vexed because Sister was a-going to cut my frock.

JULY 22. Part of this day I did not improve my time well.

JULY 30. I was careless and lost my needle.

AUG. 5. I spilt some coffee on the table.

staise
stays, part of a girl's or woman's underclothing

WHITE LEAF

JULY 8. I went and said my Catechism to-day. Came home and wrote down the questions and answers, then dressed and went to the dance, endeavoured to behave myself decent.

JULY 11. I improved my time before breakfast; after breakfast made some biscuits and did all my work before the sun was down.

JULY 12. I went to meeting and paid good attention to the sermon, came home and wrote down as much of it as I could remember. . . .

JULY 27. I did everything this morning same as usual, went to school and endeavoured to be diligent; came home and washed the butter and assisted in getting coffee.

JULY 28. I endeavoured to be diligent to-day in my learning, went from school to sit up with the sick, nursed her as well as I could.

"July 10. Spoke in haste to my little Sister."

JULY 30. I was pretty diligent at my work to-day and made a pudding for dinner.

midlin
(middling)
moderately, fairly

AUG. 1. I got some peaches for to stew after I was done washing up the things and got my work and was midlin Diligent.

—*Quoted in Shirley Glubok, editor,* Home and Child Life in Colonial Days. *New York: Macmillan, 1969.*

THINK ABOUT THIS

1. How would you describe the wrongdoings that Sumner lists? Do they seem like serious faults?
2. What kinds of things does she consider to be good or proper deeds?
3. What might Sumner have learned about herself by reading her journal?

A Boy's Letter to His Father

In the colonies, educated people wrote many letters. Husbands and wives often wrote each other letters, even when they were not separated. So did parents and children. A nine-year-old Massachusetts boy named John Quincy Adams wrote this letter to his father, the lawyer and Patriot John Adams, who was part of the Continental Congress meeting in Philadelphia during the Revolutionary War. Twenty years later the father would become the second president of the United States, and in 1825 the son would become the sixth president. The letter, written long before those public events, shows the respectful affection of the son for the father. It also shows how important education and self-improvement were in the Adams household.

BRAINTREE, JUNE THE 2ND, 1777

Dear Sir:

I love to receive letters very well, much better than I love to write them. I make but a poor figure at composition, my head is much too fickle, my thoughts are running after bird's eggs, play, and trifles until I get vexed with myself. I have but just entered the 3rd vol. of Smollett tho' I had design'd to have got it half through by this time. I have determined this week to be more diligent, as Mr. Thaxter will be absent at Court, & I cannot persue my other studies. I have set myself a Stent & determine to read the Volume Half out. If I can but keep my resolution, I will write again at the end of the week and give a better account of myself. I wish, Sir, you would give me some instructions with regard to my time & advise me how to proportion my Studies & my Play, in writing I will keep them by me & endeavour to follow them. I am, dear Sir, with a present determination of growing better yours. P.S. Sir, if you will be so good as to favour me with a Blank Book, I will transcribe the most remarkable occurrences I meet with in my reading which will serve to fix them upon my mind.

stent
stint, or amount of work to be completed in a given time

—*Reprinted in Alice Morse Earle,* Child Life in Colonial Days.
New York: Macmillan, 1899.

THINK ABOUT THIS

1. What criticisms does the letter writer make of his own behavior?

2. How does he think his father can help him improve?

Chapter 7

Religion

RELIGIOUS FREEDOM WAS ONE REASON people came to the North American colonies, and for many colonists religion played a central part in life. This was certainly true for the Pilgrims and Puritans who left the Church of England to settle the Massachusetts colony (a few also went to Virginia and Maryland). They believed they had two missions: to preach their form of Christianity to others, both Christian and non-Christian, and to promote their own spiritual growth through obedience to God's word and will. Not everyone who lived in Puritan communities was a Puritan, but ministers and church leaders had high status, and the church—which came to be known as the Congregational church—had considerable power over local affairs.

Nearly everyone in British North America believed in some form of supernatural power that individuals could harness. Certain people were suspected of being witches, able to use such power to harm others. The suspects were often older women, the poor, or people who challenged the existing social order in some way. Often these "witches" were seen simply as "wise women" who

British-born preacher George Whitefield toured the American colonies several times in the mid-eighteenth century. His sermons fueled the Great Awakening, a wave of religious excitement that swept through the colonies.

supplied the community with practical assistance in the form of herbal medicines and with harmless "magic" such as fortune-telling. At times, however, the community took a darker view of the suspected witches, saying that they had obtained their powers from the Devil. People accused of witchcraft could be punished or executed, usually with the encouragement of local religious leaders. An outbreak of feverish accusations in Salem, Massachusetts, in 1692 led to dozens of executions. Soon accusations and trials were under way in neighboring towns. Writes historian Frances Hill, "The witchcraft hysteria . . . wrecked eastern Massachusetts as would a civil war."

In the middle of the eighteenth century, colonial Puritans and other Protestant Christians experienced a religious revival called the Great Awakening. Led by powerful preachers and inspiring writers, this movement encouraged a return to the strict, strong faith of earlier times. Many new churches were founded in the colonies during the Great Awakening.

The majority of colonists were Protestant Christians, but other religions were represented in the colonies, too. The first Jews in the colonies arrived in New Amsterdam in 1654. The Jewish community grew in New Netherland, and when the colony came into British hands as New York, the community continued to flourish. Jews in New York had the right to vote, hold office, and worship. By the end of the colonial period the Jewish population numbered somewhere around three thousand people, mostly in New York, Pennsylvania, Rhode Island, South Carolina, and Georgia. Roman Catholics were concentrated in Maryland. Catholic communities also took root in Delaware and New Jersey. A few Catholics lived in Pennsylvania, although they could not vote or hold office there (neither could Jews). Finally, elements of traditional African and Native American religious belief lingered among some of the colonies' nonwhite inhabitants, although many of them adopted Christianity.

The Trial of Anne Hutchinson

The Pilgrims and Puritans came to Massachusetts to practice their religion freely, but they did not allow general religious freedom. Puritan ministers and civic leaders monitored everyone in their settlements for proper behavior such as churchgoing, and they punished anyone whose beliefs or practices did not meet their standards. These unfortunate people were fined, whipped, and sometimes banished, or forced to leave the colony. The Puritans hanged a Quaker woman, Mary Dyer, for nothing more than proclaiming her religious beliefs in Massachusetts. Another woman who came into conflict with the Puritan leaders was Anne Hutchinson, who was not afraid to speak her mind. Soon after Hutchinson and her husband arrived in Massachusetts from England in 1634, women began gathering in her home to pray and talk about religion. Hutchinson believed that God could speak to anyone, not just ministers, and that people could read and interpret the Bible for themselves. This alarmed the Puritan ministers and leaders, who were especially outraged because Hutchinson was a woman—and women were not supposed to have ideas of their own or to challenge men's authority. In 1637 Deputy Governor John Winthrop and other leaders tried Hutchinson for the crime of heresy, or differing with established religious authority. The trial ended in

A nineteenth-century engraving depicts Anne Hutchinson before the Puritan judges and critics who drove her from Massachusetts for speaking her mind on religious subjects.

banishment for Hutchinson and her family, who moved to Rhode Island. In this passage from the trial, Winthrop accuses Hutchinson of publicly claiming to receive the spirit or word of God directly, without the help of a minister. Hutchinson defends herself with energy and wit, which probably turned Winthrop against her all the more.

WINTHROP: You have not the right to question, you are but to answer the statement, that you made testimony, in public, that God spoke to you directly.

HUTCHINSON: I was on board a ship, not yet in the public colony.

WINTHROP: There were naught but Puritan colonists there.

HUTCHINSON: But the Reverend Cotton, whose son Seaborn was born aboard the *Griffin,* the voyage previous, did not have his son baptized at sea, writing me saying it was not seemly. Not because he would have to use salt water, but that he was not on consecrated ground!

WITNESS: Please the Court, I knew Mistress Hutchinson in Alford. One day in a churchyard she did tell me God spoke to her of the death of two children in that one year, and so it happened.

WINTHROP: A churchyard is a public place.

HUTCHINSON: Sir, it is. Although there be mostly those that cannot hear.

WINTHROP: A public place!

• • •

. . . *WINTHROP:* How do you know God revealed these things to you and not the Devil?

HUTCHINSON: I did not confess to either, in public. But how did Abraham know it was God's voice when He commanded him to sacrifice his only son, Isaac, and how did Abraham then know it was God's voice that stayed the knife?

WINTHROP: God spoke to the prophet Abraham and so He will speak straightaway with Mistress Hutchinson. . . . Remember, you are not to ask questions.

—*Quoted in Deborah Crawford,* Four Women in a Violent Time. *New York: Crown, 1970.*

THINK ABOUT THIS

1. Do you agree that the Puritans had the right to control the beliefs of those who settled in their colony?
2. The question of whether Anne voiced her religious beliefs in public— why would that have been important to the Puritan leaders?
3. What do you imagine was the tone of Winthrop's final remark in this passage?

"Miracles" and "Accidents": A Letter from Cotton Mather

The Mather family played a leading role in the religious and civic life of the Massachusetts colony. Richard Mather, a Puritan teacher and preacher, came from England to Massachusetts in 1635. His son, Increase Mather, was a prominent preacher and president of Harvard College. In the third generation, Cotton Mather also became a preacher. He believed in supernatural occurrences and in 1689 published a book about witchcraft and possession by evil spirits. Some historians think he stirred up the fears that led to the Salem witch trials in the early 1690s. This letter, which Mather wrote to another clergyman while the trials were taking place, talks about the confessions of some accused witches. It also discusses an earthquake that destroyed the town of Port-Royal, a notorious pirate hangout in the British Caribbean island colony of Jamaica.

"Five Witches were Lately Executed."

BOSTON, AUGT. 5, 1692.

Reverend Sir,—Our Good God is working of Miracles.

Five Witches were Lately Executed, impudently demanding of God, a Miraculous Vindication of their Innocency. Immediately upon this, Our God Miraculously sent in Five Andover-Witches, who made a most ample, surprising, amazing Confession, of all their Villainies and declared the Five newly executed to have been of their Company; discovering many more; but all agreeing in Burroughs being their Ringleader, who, I suppose, this Day receives his Trial at Salem, whither a Vast Concourse of people is gone; my Father, this morning among the Rest. Since those, there have come in other Confessors; yea, they come in daily. About this prodigious matter my Soul has been Refreshed with some Little short of Miraculous Answers of prayer; which are not to bee written; but they comfort mee with a prospect of an hopeful Issue.

Lecture
church service

Tyrius
Latin for Tyre, a wealthy Mediterranean Sea port in ancient times

Sodom
city mentioned in the Bible as the home of sinful people

The whole Town yesterday, turned the Lecture into a Fast, kept in our meeting-house; God give a Good Return. But in the morning wee were Entertained with the horrible Tidings of the Late Earthquake at Jamaica, on the 7th of June Last. When, on a fair Day, the sea suddenly swell'd, and the Earth shook, and broke in many places; and in a Minutes time, the Rich Town of Port-Royal, the *Tyrius* of the whole English America, but a very Sodom for Wickedness, was immediately swallow'd up, and the sea came Rolling over the Town. No less than seventeen hundred souls of that one Town, are missing; besides other Incredible Devastations all over the Island, where Houses are Demolished, Mountains overturned, Rocks Rent, and all manner of Destruction inflicted. The N.C. Minister there, scap'd wonderfully with his Life. Some of our poor N.E. people are Lost in the Ruines, and others have their Bones broke. Forty Vessels, were sunk, namely all whose Cables did not break; but no N.E. ones. Behold, an Accident speaking to all our English America.

I live in Pains, and want your prayers. Bestow them, dear Sir, on Your

C. Mather

—*Cotton Mather*, Diary of Cotton Mather, Volume 1.
New York: Frederick Ungar, n.d.

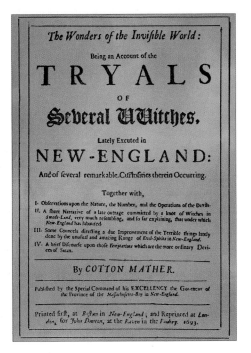

The *Wonders of the Invisible World:*

Being an Account of the

T R Y A L S

OF

Several Witches.

Lately Executed in

NEW-ENGLAND:

And of several remarkable Curiosities therein Occurring.

Together with,

I. Observations upon the Nature, the Number, and the Operations of the Devils.
II. A short Narrative of a late outrage committed by a knot of Witches in Swede-Land, very much resembling, and so far explaining, that under which New-England has laboured.
III. Some Councils directing a due Improvement of the Terrible things lately done by the unusual and amazing Range of Evil-Spirits in New-England.
IV. A brief Discourse upon those Temptations which are the more ordinary Devices of Satan.

By COTTON MATHER.

Published by the Special Command of his EXCELLENCY the Governour of the Province of the Massachusetts-Bay in New-England.

Printed first, at Boston in New-England; and Reprinted at London, for John Dunton, at the Raven in the Poultry. 1693.

THINK ABOUT THIS

1. Why does Mather regard the confessions of the five accused witches from Andover as a miracle?

2. Mather says that Jamaica earthquake was "speaking to all America." What do you think he imagined it was saying?

After the Witch Trials: An Accuser Changes Her Mind

In 1692, twelve-year-old Ann Putnam was one of the chief accusers in the Salem witch trials. Her fits and shrieks led to the hanging of men and women, including members of the Nurse family, her neighbors, as witches. Fourteen years later, Putnam became a member of the congregation of Salem Village church. She stood before the other members while the preacher read this confession to the congregation. It refers to the terrible events of the

This edition of Cotton Mather's *Wonders of the Invisible World*, published in London in 1693, discusses the tragic withcraft hysteria and trials that had just taken place in Salem.

The Salem witch trials, shown here in a nineteenth-century engraving, were based on accusations from unreliable and confused young people. Colonial leaders later admitted that the trials had been a ghastly mistake.

witch trials, which had come to be viewed as a dreadful mistake based on false accusations. Putnam seems to have felt true regret for what she had done. Still, she placed the blame for the deaths on something outside her rather than on her own human weaknesses, which might have included confusion, jealousy, anger, or the childish thrill of becoming suddenly powerful.

I DESIRE TO BE HUMBLED BEFORE GOD for that sad and humbling providence that befell my father's family in the year about '92; that

I, being then in my childhood, should, by such a providence of God, be made an instrument for the accusing of several persons of a grievous crime, whereby their lives were taken away from them, whom now I have just grounds and good reason to believe they were innocent persons; and that it was a great delusion of Satan that deceived me in that sad time, whereby I justly fear I have been instrumental, with others, though ignorantly and unwittingly, to bring upon myself and this land the guilt of innocent blood; though what was said or done by me against any person I can truly and uprightly say, before God and man, I did it not out of any anger, malice, or ill-will to any person, for I had no such thing against any one of them; but what I did was ignorantly, being deluded by Satan. And particularly, as I was a chief instrument of accusing Goodwife Nurse and her two sisters, I desire to lie in the dust, and to be humbled for it, in that I was a cause, with others, of so sad a calamity to them and their families; for which I desire to lie in the dust, and earnestly beg forgiveness of God, and from all those unto whom I have given just cause of sorrow and offence, whose relations were taken away or accused.

" . . . their lives were taken away from them . . . now I have just grounds and good reason to believe they were innocent persons."

—*Quoted in Frances Hill,* A Delusion of Satan: The Full Story of the Salem Witch Trials. *New York: Doubleday, 1995.*

THINK ABOUT THIS

1. Why do you think Ann Putnam made this confession?
2. What does Putnam say was the cause of the false accusations she made?

The Great Awakening:
A Minister Warns Sinners of Their Fate

Jonathan Edwards (1703–1758) was the leading religious figure of the Great Awakening, the religious movement that swept over colonial America in the middle of the eighteenth century. From early childhood Edwards was trained for a career in the church. He was a teacher, pastor, missionary, and college president who carried Puritan ideas and beliefs into the eighteenth century. His 1741 sermon "Sinners in the Hands of an Angry God" was meant to raise fear in the hearts of those who were not sincere in their beliefs. In Edwards's view, you didn't have to commit a crime to be a sinner—all it took was for your faith to be lazy or weak.

THE GOD THAT HOLDS YOU over the pit of hell, much as one holds a spider, or some loathsome insect, over the fire, abhors you, and is dreadfully provoked; his wrath towards you burns like fire; he looks upon you as worthy of nothing else, but to be cast into the fire; he is of purer eyes than to bear to have you in his sight; you are ten thousand times so abominable in his eyes as the most venomous serpent is in ours. You have offended him infinitely more than ever a stubborn rebel did his prince: and yet 'tis nothing but his hand that holds you from falling into the fire every moment: 'tis to be ascribed to nothing else, that you did not go to hell the last night; that you was suffered to awake again in this world, after you closed your eyes to sleep: and there is no other reason to be given why you have not dropped into hell since you arose in the morning, but that God's hand has held you up: and there is no other reason to be given why you han't gone to hell since you have sat here in the house of God, provoking his

"Oh sinner! Consider the fearful danger you are in."

Jonathan Edwards tried to rekindle the spirit of Puritan devotion. One of his main themes was the terrible fate awaiting those whose faith was not as strong as he thought it should be.

pure eyes by your sinful wicked manner of attending his solemn worship: yea, there is nothing else that is to be given as a reason why you don't this very moment drop down into hell.

O sinner! Consider the fearful danger you are in: 'tis a great furnace of wrath, a wide and bottomless pit, full of the fire of wrath, that you are held over in the hand of that God, whose wrath is provoked and incensed as much against you as against any of the damned in hell: you hang by a slender thread, with the flames of divine wrath flashing about it, and ready every moment to singe it, and burn it asunder; and you have no interest in any mediator, and nothing to lay hold of to save yourself, nothing to keep off the flames of wrath, nothing of your own, nothing that you have ever done, nothing that you can do, to induce God to spare you one moment.

—*John Smith, Harry Stout, and Kenneth Minkema, editors,* A Jonathan Edwards Reader. *New Haven, CT: Yale University Press, 1995.*

THINK ABOUT THIS

1. According to Edwards, what is the only thing that keeps sinners from falling into hell?

2. Why do you think Edwards used so many images of fire to describe a sinner's fate?

3. Why do you think Edwards believed that a slackening of faith would necessarily cause a person to sin?

Chapter 8

Learning and Culture

SETTLERS IN NORTH AMERICA had their hands full carving out homesteads in the wilderness, feeding and clothing themselves and their families, dealing with the Native Americans, and building social and political institutions. Still, many of them managed to find time for at least some education.

New England led the way in educational achievement, partly because the Puritans placed a high value on literacy, the ability to read and write. As early as 1647 they made a law requiring each community with fifty or more families to have a teacher whose salary would be paid with taxes. Nearly three-fourths of all New England men and about half of the women in the region were literate. Other parts of the colonies were not so quick to establish public education. Some of the wealthiest colonists sent their children to private academies, or even to England, for instruction. But many colonists, especially the rural population, learned to read and write at home, taught by their parents with a Bible as a schoolbook, or had only a few years or even months of formal education.

The colonists who came to North America brought literature,

The coffeehouse was an important social institution in eighteenth-century England and America. There men gathered to read the news and discuss the issues of the day.

music, and the arts with them from their parent countries, but not all culture was imported from across the sea. New talents sprouted from American soil. Many colonial writers dealt with religious subjects. Books of sermons were popular, as were books in which people described their own spiritual growth. Some colonists, recognizing that the settling of North America was a historic event, wrote accounts of the founding and early years of their colonies. Examples include William Penn's *A Further Account of the Province of Pennsylvania* (1685) and Robert Beverley's *The History and Present State of Virginia* (1705).

One of the most popular forms of colonial writing was the Indian captivity narrative, true stories—or mostly so—whose authors described being captured and held prisoner by Native Americans. *The Redeemed Captive Returning unto Zion* (1707) was a widely read captivity narrative by John Williams, minister of Deerfield, Massachusetts, whose whole community was killed or captured in 1704. Because such stories were supposed to show how God rescued faithful believers and returned them to civilization, Williams did not tell the complete story of his eight-year-old daughter, Eunice, who became a full member of the Indian community during her captivity and later married an Indian man, refusing to return to white society.

The North American colonies also produced inventors such as Joseph Jenkes, who in 1646 obtained the first patent granted in the colonies, for a water-powered mill he had designed; scientists such as John and William Bartram (who studied plants); and painters such as Benjamin West, who immortalized great moments in colonial history with works such as *The Death of Wolfe* (about the French and Indian War) and *Penn's Treaty with the Indians* (about William Penn's treaty of peace with the Native Americans of Pennsylvania). The colonies contained their share of creativity, imagination, and inspiration, as the achievement of these and many others show.

America's First Woman Writer Dedicates Words of Wisdom to Her Son

Eighteen-year-old newlywed Anne Dudley Bradstreet came to Massachusetts with other English Puritans in 1630. Twenty years later, an English publisher issued a book of her poetry. It was called *The Tenth Muse, Lately Sprung Up in America*. According to the ancient Greeks, the Muses were nine goddesses who inspired poetry, music, and all art and learning—Bradstreet's publisher was calling her the tenth Muse. Bradstreet's poems reveal her deep religious faith and also, occasionally, her impatience with people who felt that she should devote herself to "women's work" such as sewing rather than to writing. The following passages are from her book *Meditations*. She dedicated these thoughts to her son, saying, "You once desired me to leave something for you in writing that you might look upon when you should see me no more."

YOUTH IS THE TIME of getting, middle age of improving, and old age of spending; a negligent youth is usually attended by an ignorant middle age, and both by an empty old age. He that hath nothing to feed on but vanity and lies must needs lie down in the Bed of sorrow.

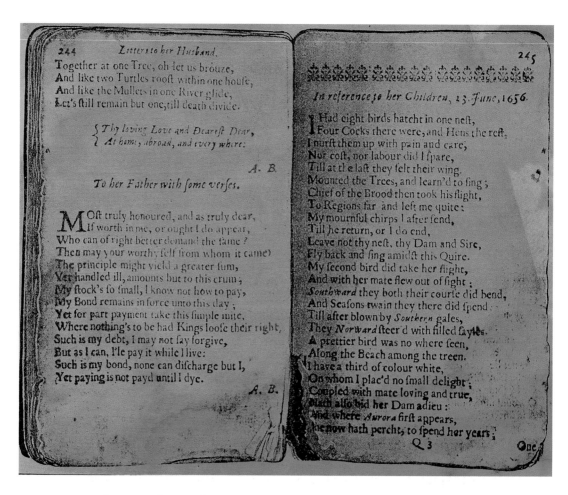

A page from an edition of Anne Bradstreet's poetry published in Boston in 1678.

If we had no winter the spring would not be so pleasant: if we did not sometimes taste of adversity, prosperity would not be so welcome.

All weak and diseased bodies have hourly mementos of their mortality. But the soundest of men have likewise their nightly monitor by the emblem of death, which is their sleep (for so is death often called), and not only their death, but the grave is lively represented before their eyes, by beholding their bed; the morning may mind them of the resurrection; and the sun approaching, of the appearing of the Sun of righteousness, at whose coming they shall all rise out of their beds, the long night shall fly away, and the day of eternity shall never end: seeing these things must be, what manner of persons ought we to be, in all good conversation?

—*John Harvard Ellis, editor,* The Works of Anne Bradstreet in Prose and Verse. *Charlestown, MA: 1867.*

THINK ABOUT THIS

How do you think Bradstreet would answer the question she asks in her final sentence?

"The Surest Foundation of Happiness": Benjamin Franklin on Education

During the course of the eighteenth century, Benjamin Franklin dipped into almost every part of intellectual and public life in the colonies. He owed his livelihood to the printed word: He wrote and printed newspapers, pamphlets, and books, and he owned eighteen paper mills. Born in 1706, by the age of forty-two he was wealthy enough to dedicate the rest of his long life to what he called "philosophical studies and amusement." Franklin turned his attention to scientific experiments, writing, civic projects, and politics. Later in life he would help the newly formed United States win the support of France. Long before he rose to national fame, he took an interest in the affairs of Philadelphia, his home city. In 1749 he published "Proposals Relating to the Education of Youth in Pensilvania," a call for help in establishing an academy, or

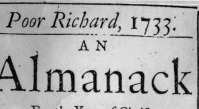

Poor Richard, 1733.

AN

Almanack

For the Year of Chrift

1733,

Being the Firſt after LEAP YEAR:

And makes ſince the Creation	Years
By the Account of the Eaſtern Greeks	7241
By the Latin Church, when ☉ ent. ♈	6932
By the Computation of W.W.	5742
By the Roman Chronology	5682
By the Jewiſh Rabbies	5494

Wherein is contained

The Lunations, Eclipſes, Judgment of the Weather, Spring Tides, Planets Motions & mutual Aſpects, Sun and Moon's Riſing and Setting, Length of Days, Time of High Water, Fairs, Courts, and obſervable Days.

Fitted to the Latitude of Forty De and a Meridian of Five Hours Weſt fr but may without ſenſible Error, ſer jacent Places, even from Newfoun Carolina.

By RICHARD SAUNDE

PHILADELP
Printed and ſold by B. FRANI
Printing-Office near tl

school. He was successful—two years later the academy opened. Today it is the University of Pennsylvania.

ADVERTISEMENT TO THE READER

It has long been regretted as a misfortune to the youth of this province, that we have no ACADEMY, in which they might receive the accomplishments of a regular education. . . . Those who incline to favour the design with their advice, either as to the parts of learning to be taught, the order of study, the method of teaching, the economy of the school, or any other matter of importance to the success of the undertaking, are desired to communicate their sentiments as soon as may be, by letter directed to B. FRANKLIN, *Printer,* in PHILADELPHIA.

PROPOSALS

The good education of youth has been esteemed by wise men in all ages, as the surest foundation of the happiness both of private families and of commonwealths. Almost all governments have therefore made it a principal object of their attention, to establish and endow with proper revenues, such seminaries of learning, as might supply the succeed-

This portrait of Benjamin Franklin is based on a drawing made of him in Paris in 1777, when he was seventy-one years old. *Poor Richard's Almanack,* first published in 1733, was Franklin's best-known work, a blend of practical information and inspirational sayings.

ing age with men qualified to serve the publick with honour to themselves, and to their country.

Many of the first settlers of these provinces were men who had received a good education in *Europe,* and to their wisdom and good management we owe much of our present prosperity. But their hands were full, and they could not do all things. The present race are not thought to be generally of equal ability: For though the *American* youth are allowed not to want capacity; yet the best capacities require cultivation, it being truly with them, as with the best ground, which unless well tilled and sowed with profitable seed, produces only ranker weeds. . . .

" . . . the best capacities require cultivation."

—*Reprinted in Esmond Wright, editor,* Benjamin Franklin: His Life As He Wrote It. *Cambridge, MA: Harvard University Press, 1990.*

THINK ABOUT THIS

1. According to Franklin, why is education valuable to communities and countries as well as to individuals and their families?
2. Why does Franklin think that the new generation of Americans has less ability than the founders of the colonies?

A Matter of Musical Taste: An Anonymous Letter

Many kinds of music, song, and dance existed in the colonies. Some musical traditions were based on old folk tunes and dance steps from England, songs that all country people could sing. Others drew upon trained musicians and written compositions. Africans in the colonies had their own traditions, such as the banjo, an instrument they brought from Africa that originally consisted of a hollow gourd and strings of catgut. African music and dance appealed to some white colonists, although others thought it was unseemly for white people to enjoy "primitive" music. Philip Vickers Fithian, the young missionary who traveled through the Virginia and Pennsylvania colonies and wrote about backcountry life, was disgusted by the fact that two young men he knew sometimes slipped away from their duties to play music and dance with the black servants. Another sort of problem arose in churches when young people adopted new ways of singing traditional hymns. Some people grew so upset with such changes that they switched to other churches. One historian who surveyed early church records in the Massachusetts colony found that nearly a fifth of the churches lost members because of changes in their musical practices.

" . . . a light, airy, Jiggish Tune, better adapted to a Country Dance, than to the awful Business of Chanting forth the Praises of the King of Kings."

This anonymous letter printed in the *New Hampshire Gazette* of January 13, 1764, shows how strongly people could feel about church singing.

THERE ARE A SET OF GENIUSES, who stick themselves up in a Gallery, and seem to think that they have a Priviledge of engrossing all the singing to themselves; and truely they take away a very effectual method to secure this Priviledge, namely by singing such Tunes, as is impossible for the Congregation to join in. Whom they get to compose for them, or whether they compose for themselves, I will not pretend to determine; but, instead of those plain and easy Compositions which are essential to the Awful

Solemnity of Church Music, away they get off, one after another, in a light, airy, Jiggish Tune, better adapted to a Country Dance, than to the awful Business of Chanting forth the Praises of the King of Kings.

—*Quoted in Jacob Ernest Cooke, editor,* Encyclopedia of the North American Colonies, Volume 3. *New York: Scribner's, 1993.*

THINK ABOUT THIS

Why do you think the writer of this complaint disliked the music that was being sung in his or her church?

The Colonies' Leading Physician: Benjamin Rush Recalls His Practice

Benjamin Rush was born into a Quaker family on a farm near Philadelphia in 1745. After studying medicine in the colonies and in Edinburgh, Scotland, he began practicing as a doctor in Philadelphia. In addition to becoming one of the foremost scientific men of the colonies and a leading medical teacher, Rush was a

Remembered as one of the signers of the Declaration of Independence, Benjamin Rush was the best and most respected doctor in the American colonies.

Patriot who supported American liberty and signed the Declaration of Independence. In 1800 he began writing the story of his own life for his children. This passage tells how he started out in medical practice.

I HAD BEEN MUCH STRUCK in reading when a boy, that Dr. Boerhaave [a famous European medical teacher] had said that "the poor were his best patients, because God was their paymaster". . . . My natural disposition made this mode of getting into business very agreeable to me, for I had a natural sympathy with distress of every kind. My conduct during my apprenticeship moreover paved the way for my success in adopting it, for I had made myself acceptable at that time to the poor by my services to them. I began business among them. . . . From the time of my settlement in Philadelphia in 1769 'till 1775 I led a life of constant labor and self-denial. My shop was crowded with the poor in the morning and at meal times, and nearly every street and alley was visited by me every day. There are few old huts now standing in the ancient parts of the city in which I have not attended sick people. Often have I ascended the upper story of these huts by a ladder, and many hundred times have been obliged to rest my weary limbs upon the bedside of the sick (from the want of chairs) where I was sure I risqued not only taking their disease but being infected by vermin. More than once did I suffer from the latter. Nor did I hasten from these abodes of poverty. Where no other help was attainable, I have often remained in them long eno' to adminster my prescriptions, particularly bleeding and glysters, with my own hands. I review these scenes with heartfelt pleasure. I believed at the time

"... 'the poor were his best patients, because God was their paymaster.'"

that they would not lose their reward. "Take care of him and I will repay thee" were words which I have repeated many times to myself in leaving the rooms of this class of sick people. Nor have I been disappointed. Here therefore will I set my seal to the truth of the divine promises to such acts of duty. To His goodness in accepting my services to His poor children I ascribe the innumerable blessings of my life; nay, more, my life itself.

—*Reprinted in George W. Corner, editor,* The Autobiography of Benjamin Rush. *Princeton, NJ: Princeton University Press, 1948.*

THINK ABOUT THIS

What reasons does Rush give for devoting so much time and energy to treating the poor?

A Slave Finds Her Voice

Phillis Wheatley was brought from Africa to America as a slave in 1761, when she was seven or eight years old. Her master and mistress allowed her to be educated and encouraged her to become a Christian and a writer. Wheatley's poems, first published in Boston in 1770, were much admired in her own day, and she was treated as something of a celebrity on a visit to England. Wheatley wrote in the flowery language that writers used in the eighteenth century, and many of her poems were written in honor of particular events such as funerals or journeys. In this poem, Wheatley addresses a young black painter and praises his work.

Phillis Wheatley was one of the few colonial slaves to find a public voice. This illustration of her appeared in an edition of her poems published in London in 1773.

TO S. M., A YOUNG AFRICAN PAINTER, ON SEEING HIS WORK

To show the lab'ring bosom's deep intent,
And thought in living characters to paint.
When first thy pencil did those beauties give,
And breathing figures learnt from thee to live,
How did those prospects give my soul delight,
A new creation rushing on my sight?

Still, wond'rous youth! each noble path pursue,
On deathless glories fix thine ardent view:
Still may the painter's and the poet's fire
To aid thy pencil and thy verse conspire!
And may the charms of each seraphic theme
Conduct thy footsteps to immortal fame!
High to the blissful wonders of the skies
Elate the soul, and raise thy wishful eyes.

—*Reprinted in C. Herbert Renfro, editor,* Life and Works of Phillis Wheatley. *Washington, DC: Pendleton, 1916.*

"Still may the painter's and the poet's fire To aid thy pencil and thy verse conspire!"

THINK ABOUT THIS

If Wheatley's poem is addressed to a painter and not to a poet, why do you think she speaks of "the painter's and the poet's fire" and "thy pencil and thy verse"?

The 1775 battles of Lexington and Concord marked the beginning of the American struggle for independence. In this illustration, made that year, British Redcoats assemble their forces at Concord.

Toward Independence

PEOPLE WHO SETTLED in the colonies did so with the permission of the British crown and they understood that they were part of Britain's realm. They obeyed British laws, and although each colony had some form of local government, overall authority rested with governors who were appointed by the king or queen or by Parliament, the British lawmaking body. Although some of the colonists wanted to create new kinds of communities or social organizations, they did not dream of forming independent new nations.

After the middle of the eighteenth century, however, some people in British North America began questioning the relationship of the colonies to the parent country. They argued that the colonists deserved more control over their government and that Britain was trampling their rights. Some of these ideas reflected the Enlightenment, a wave of political, scientific, and philosophical thought that swept through Europe and North America. People in America were especially influenced by the ideas of political philosopher John Locke, who wrote about what he called the social contract. Locke

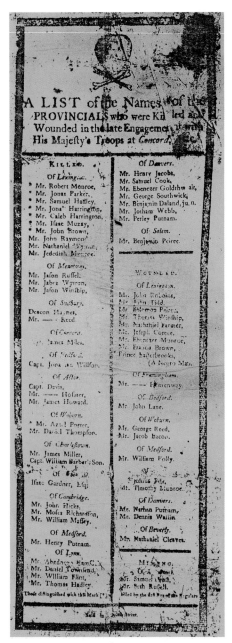

In the era before radio and television, people relied on the printed word for news. This handbill, or poster, listed the "Provincials" (colonists) killed or wounded at Lexington and Concord.

claimed that individuals created governments to protect their lives, their liberty, and their property. If a government threatened those rights, it broke the social contract, which meant that the people could change or even unmake the government. American colonists began to absorb the idea that people had a right to rebel against unjust rule.

After the end of the French and Indian War in 1763, various injustices vexed the colonists. In an attempt to prevent fights with the Indians, Britain decided to station a large military force in the colonies. The colonists were expected to pay for this force and even, in some cases, to house the soldiers. And by declaring that settlers from the colonies could not cross the Appalachian Mountains, Parliament made many Americans feel that their freedom was being unfairly limited.

Matters worsened as Parliament passed a series of trade laws meant to raise money from the colonies, in part to pay the costs of the French and Indian War. Colonists reacted with surprise, indignation, and eventually fury to new taxes and fees. They resented having their tax money cross the

Atlantic to be spent by a Parliament to which they could not elect representatives. During the 1760s American opposition to the new taxes reached a fever pitch. People refused to buy imported British goods; women organized groups called the Daughters of Liberty to encourage the use of American-made cloth and household items. Officials who tried to enforce the new taxes were attacked. The cry "No taxation without representation!" rang out in the streets.

Some colonists were now talking not just of an adjustment in the colonies' relationship with Britain but of a major change, perhaps even a break. The colonists began to fall into two camps: Loyalists who wanted to retain the old relationship with Britain, and Patriots who wanted to uphold American rights whatever the cost. Tension grew until in April of 1775, at Lexington and Concord in Massachusetts, fighting broke out between British troops and colonial militiamen, or citizen soldiers. Although the colonies did not declare their independence from Great Britain until more than a year later, those shots were really the beginning of the Revolutionary War and the end of colonial America.

In 1765 the British government issued this stamp for use in the colonies. The Stamp Act, which required people to pay to have the stamp applied to various goods, infuriated colonists and became one of the causes of their eventual revolt.

Virginia's Leaders Scorn the Stamp Act

In 1619 the Virginia colony took the first step toward American self-government when the governor gave the colonists some say in local government. They formed the House of Burgesses, the oldest American legislature. That legislature, later called the General Assembly, met in 1765 to discuss the Stamp Act, which required colonists to pay for an official stamp on most printed materials. Patrick Henry, a patriotic firebrand, called the act a mistake on the part of King George III. Referring to Roman and English rulers who had been assassinated, Henry cried out, "Caesar had his Brutus, Charles the First his Cromwell, and George the Third may profit from their example"—meaning that George should avoid enraging a possible assassin. To those who said that such speech was treason against the king, Henry replied, "If this be treason, make the most of it." Not all of Virginia's assemblymen approved of Henry's strong words, but the group prepared a list of resolves, or statements, to send to the king. These resolves reject the Stamp Act, and they also clearly state that the General Assembly does not recognize the king's or Parliament's right to tax Virginia. In the end, however, the assembly did not approve the resolves or send them to the king.

RESOLVED, That the first adventurers and settlers of this His Majesty's Colony and Dominion of Virginia brought with them, and transmitted to their posterity, and all other His Majesty's subjects since inhabiting in this His Majesty's said Colony, all the liberties, privileges, franchises, and immunities, that have at any time been held, enjoyed, and possessed, by the people of Great Britain.

Resolved, That by two royal charters, granted by King James the First, the colonists aforesaid are declared entitled to all liberties, privileges, and immunities of denizens and natural subjects, to all intents and purposes, as if they had been abiding and born within the realm of England.

Resolved, That the taxation of the people by themselves, or by persons chosen by themselves to represent them, who can only know what taxes the people are able to bear, or the easiest method of raising them, and must themselves be affected by every tax laid on the people, is the only security against a burthensome taxation, and the distinguishing characteristick of British freedom, without which the ancient constitution cannot exist.

Resolved, That His Majesty's liege people of this his most ancient and loyal Colony have without interruption enjoyed the inestimable right of being governed by such laws, respecting their internal polity and taxation, as are derived from their own consent; and that the same hath never been forfeited or yielded up, but hath been consistently recognized by the kings and people of Great Britain.

"... the inhabitants of this Colony, are not bound to yield obedience to any law or ordinance whatever... other than the laws or ordinances of the General Assembly."

Resolved therefore, That the General Assembly of this Colony have the only and sole exclusive right and power to lay taxes and impositions upon the inhabitants of this colony, and that every attempt to vest such power in any person or persons whatsoever other than the General Assembly aforesaid has a manifest tendency to destroy British as well as American freedom.

Resolved, That His Majesty's liege people, the inhabitants of this Colony, are not bound to yield obedience to any law or ordinance whatever, designed to impose any taxation whatsoever upon them, other than the laws or ordinances of the General Assembly aforesaid.

Resolved, That any person who shall, by speaking or writing, assert or maintain that any person or persons other than the General

Assembly of this Colony, have any right or power to impose or lay any taxation on the people here, shall be deemed an enemy to His Majesty's colony.

—*Reprinted in Samuel E. Morison,* Sources and Documents Illustrating the American Revolution. *Oxford, England: Clarendon Press, 1923.*

THINK ABOUT THIS

1. The writers of these resolves called taxation without representation a threat to British as well as American freedom. Why?
2. Do the writers appear to be calling for political independence from Great Britain?

A Loyalist's Ordeal: Colonists Take Sides

In 1765 Thomas Hutchinson, the chief justice and lieutenant governor of Massachusetts, was the second most powerful and important man in the colony. One August night a mob burst into his house and, with terrifying violence, took everything he owned and destroyed his home. If Hutchinson and his family had not fled, the rioters might have killed them. Many people said that that attack on Hutchinson was an expression of public disapproval of the Stamp Act and of a colonial government that took orders from the British Parliament. But others, including Hutchinson's fellow Loyalists, called the attackers simply greedy gang members and looters. Hutchinson, who later wrote a history of the Revolutionary War from the Loyalist point of view, made this statement on the day after the riot.

"I hope all will see how easily the people may be deluded, enflamed, and carried away with madness."

SENSIBLE THAT I AM INNOCENT, that all the charges against me are false, I cannot help feeling—and though I am not obliged to give an answer to all the questions that may be put me by every lawless person, yet I call GOD to witness (and I would not for a thousand worlds call my *Maker* to witness to a falsehood)—I say, I call my *Master* to witness that I never, in New England or Old, in Great Britain or America, neither directly nor indirectly, was aiding, assisting, or supporting, or in the least promoting or encouraging what is commonly called the Stamp Act, but on the contrary, did all in my power, and strove as much as in me lay, to prevent it. This is not declared through timidity, for I have nothing to fear. They can only take away my life, which is of little value when deprived of all its comforts, all that is dear to me, and nothing surrounding me but the most piercing distress.

I hope the eyes of the people will be opened, that they will see how easy it is for some designing, wicked men to spread false reports, raise suspicions and jealousies in the minds of the populace and enrage them against the innocent. But if guilty, this is

Thomas Hutchinson was the last royal governor of Massachusetts. Many colonists despised him—a feeling shown in this 1774 cartoon of the governor being punished for "crimes" against the colonies.

not the way to proceed. The laws of our country are open to punish those who have offended. This destroying all peace and order of the community—*all will feel its effects*. And I hope all will see how easily the people may be deluded, enflamed, and carried away with madness against an innocent man.

—*Quoted in Bernard Bailyn,* The Ordeal of Thomas Hutchinson. *Cambridge, MA: Harvard University Press, 1974.*

THINK ABOUT THIS

1. How do you feel about the actions taken by the mob against Hutchinson? Even if he had supported the Stamp Act, were they justified?
2. What is the warning contained in Hutchinson's statement? Do you agree?
3. Do you think Hutchinson was persuasive in his defense? Why?

Ruin or Salvation: John Adams Looks Ahead

One of the many Americans stirred up by the Stamp Act was a Boston lawyer named John Adams. His diary entries at the beginning of 1766 show that he expected the coming year to be very eventful. Britain would try to enforce the Stamp Act, and Americans would resist. The clash of wills would lead to either destructive punishment of the colonies or recognition of their rights.

In the first of these two entries, Adams describes a letter that Mr. Deberdt, a spokesman from the colonies to the British government, had written to Lord Dartmouth, the official of Parliament responsible for the Stamp Act. In the second, he describes actions taken in various colonies against the people responsible for enforcing the Act—and against any informers who reported violations of the Act to the authorities. Adams did far more than just write about the stirring events and issues of his time. Soon he would play an important role in the struggle for American independence, and later he would serve as the second president of the United States.

JANUARY 1, 1766. Wednesday. Severe cold, and a prospect of snow. We are now upon the beginning of a year of greater expectation than any that has passed before it. This year brings ruin or salvation to the British colonies. The eyes of all America are fixed on the British Parliament. In short, Britain and America are staring at each other, and they will probably stare more and more for some time.

"This year brings ruin or salvation to the British colonies."

At home all day. Mr. Joshua Hayward, Jr., dined with me; town politics the subject. Doctor Tufts here in the afternoon; American politics the subject. Read in the evening a letter from Mr. Deberdt, our present agent, to Lord Dartmouth, in which he considers three questions: 1. Whether in equity or policy America ought to refund any part of the expense of driving away the French in the last war? 2. Whether it is necessary for the defense of the British plantations to keep up an army here? 3. Whether in equity the Parliament can tax us? Each of which he discusses like a man of sense, integrity, and humanity, well informed in the nature of his subject.

. . . It is said at New York, that private letters inform [that] the great men [in Britain] are exceedingly irritated at the tumults in America, and are determined to enforce the act. This irritable race, however, will [need] good luck to enforce it. They will find it a more obstinate war than the conquest of Canada and Louisiana.

JANUARY 2. THURSDAY. A great storm of snow last night; weather tempestuous all day. Waddled through the snow driving my cattle to water at Doctor Savil's; a fine piece of glowing exercise. Brother spent the evening here in cheerful chat.

At Philadelphia, the Heart-and-Hand Fire Company has expelled Mr. Hughes, the stamp man for that colony. The freemen of Talbot county, in Maryland, have erected a gibbet before the door of the court-house, and have hanged on it the effigies of a stamp informer in chains, *in terrorem* till the Stamp Act shall be repealed; and have resolved, unanimously, to hold in utter contempt and abhorrence every stamp officer, and every favorer of the Stamp Act, and to "have no communication with any such persons, not even to speak to him, unless to upbraid him with his baseness."

So triumphant is the spirit of liberty everywhere. Such a union was never before known in America. In the wars that have been with the French and Indians a union could never be effected. . . .

in terrorem
Latin for "to frighten them"

—Reprinted in T.J. Stiles, editor, Founding Fathers in Their Own Words. *New York: Perigee, 1999.*

THINK ABOUT THIS

What feature of the Stamp Act uproar does Adams see as new in colonial history?

The Sacred Cause of Liberty: A Pennsylvania Farmer's Letter

John Dickinson was a farmer in Pennsylvania. In the late 1760s he wrote a series of letters "to the Inhabitants of the British Colonies" calling attention to what he saw as the growing threat to the colonies' liberty. Newspapers throughout the colonies printed his letters, and people excitedly discussed them in coffeehouses, taverns, and other meeting places. In this first letter, published November 5, 1767, Dickinson introduces himself and explains his devotion to the idea of freedom. The rest of the letter indignantly calls attention to the Quartering Act, a law passed by Parliament that ordered local authorities in the colonies to provide housing and supplies for royal troops, even though the New York Assembly had already refused to pay for some of the soldiers' expenses. Parliament, as Dickinson saw it, was overturning the laws of New York—something that could not be allowed to stand.

Pennsylvania farmer John Dickinson's widely published letters on political topics helped rouse the colonists against unfair British laws.

MY DEAR COUNTRYMEN,

I am a farmer, settled after a variety of fortunes near the banks of the river Delaware, in the province of Pennsylvania. I received a liberal education and have been engaged in the busy scenes of life, but am now convinced, that a man may be as happy without bustle as with it.

My farm is small, my servants are few and good, I have a little money at interest, I wish for no more, my employment in my own affairs is easy, and with a contented, grateful mind, undisturbed by worldly hopes or fears relating to myself, I am completing the number of days allotted to me by divine goodness.

Being generally master of my time, I spend a good deal of it in a library, which I think the most valuable part of my small estate; and being acquainted with two or three gentlemen of abilities and learning who honour me with their friendship, I have acquired, I believe, a greater knowledge in history and the laws and constitution of my country, than is generally attained by men of my class, many of them not being so fortunate as I have been in the opportunities of getting information.

From my infancy I was taught to love humanity and liberty. Enquiry and experience have since confirmed my reverence for the lessons then given me, by convincing me more fully of their truth and excellence. Benevolence towards mankind excites wishes for their welfare, and such wishes endear the means of fulfilling them. These can be found in liberty only, and therefore her sacred cause ought to be espoused by every man on every occasion, to the utmost of his power. As a charitable but poor person does not withhold his mite because he cannot relieve all the distress of the miserable, so should not any honest man suppress his sentiments concerning freedom, however small their influence is likely to be. Perhaps he 'may touch some wheel' that will have an effect greater than he could reasonably expect.

"From my infancy I was taught to love humanity and liberty."

These being my sentiments, I am encouraged to offer to you, my countrymen, my thoughts on some late transactions that appear to me to be of the utmost importance to you. Conscious of my own defects, I have waited some time, in expectation of seeing the subject treated by persons much better qualified for the task; but being therein disappointed, and apprehensive that longer delays will be injurious, I venture at length to request the attention of the public, praying that these lines may be read with the same zeal for the happiness of British America, with which they were wrote.

—*Reprinted in Samuel E. Morison,* Sources and Documents Illustrating the American Revolution. *Oxford, England: Clarendon Press, 1923.*

THINK ABOUT THIS

1. Why did Dickinson wait so long before making his opinion public?

2. Why did he decide to write the letter at last?

A Student Speaks Out

In the fall of 1774 the colonists created the Continental Congress. The Congress was not specifically a governing body like a legislature, but it was a political body. Its goal was to express the colonists' concerns to Great Britain and to protect their interests. Some colonists, however, disapproved of the Congress, calling it illegal and an insult to Britain. Samuel Seabury, a well-known priest, published pamphlets that criticized the Congress. He warned that it could plunge the colonists into a war they could not win. Nineteen-year-old Alexander Hamilton, a brilliant student at King's College in New York (now Columbia University), replied to Seabury in pamphlets of his own. This pamphlet was titled "A Full Vindication of the Measure of Congress," and in it Hamilton argues that the Continental Congress has a right to exist. Hamilton presents the conflict between the colonies and Britain as a question of freedom or slavery. He recognizes that war may result, but he believes that, in the end, America will win.

THE ONLY DISTINCTION BETWEEN freedom and slavery consists in this: In the former state a man is governed by the laws to which he has given his consent, either in person or by his representative; in the latter, he is governed by the will of another. In the one case, his life and property are his own; in the other, they depend upon the pleasure of his master. It is easy to discern which of these two states is preferable. No man in his senses can hesitate to be free, rather than a slave.

That Americans are entitled to freedom is incontestable on every rational principle. All men have one common original: they participate in one common nature, and consequently have one common right. No reason can be assigned why one man should exercise any power or pre-eminence over his fellow-creatures more than another; unless they have voluntarily vested him with it. Since, then, Americans have not, by any act of theirs, empowered the British Parliament to make laws for them, it follows [Parliament] can have no just authority to do it.

"That Americans are entitled to freedom is incontestable on every rational principle."

Besides the clear voice of natural justice in this respect, the fundamental principles of the English constitution are in our favor. It has been repeatedly demonstrated that the idea of legislation or taxation, when the subject is not represented, is inconsistent with *that*. Nor is this all; our charters, the express conditions on which our progenitors relinquished their native countries, and same to settle in this, precludes every claim of ruling and taxing us without our assent. . . .

What, then, is the subject of our controversy with the mother country? It is this: Whether we shall preserve the security to our lives and properties, which the laws of nature, the genius of the British constitution, and our charters afford us; or whether we shall resign them into the hands of the British House of Commons, which is no more privileged to dispose of them than the Great Mogul.

. . . It is evident that [Britain] must do something decisive. She must either listen to our complaints and restore us to a peaceful enjoyment of our violated rights, or she must exert herself to enforce her despotic claims by fire and sword. . . . Our numbers are very considerable; the courage of Americans has been tried and proved. Contests for liberty have ever been found the most bloody, implacable, and obstinate. . . . It would be a hard, if not impracticable, task to subjugate us by force.

. . . Those who affect to ridicule the resistance America might make to the military force of Great Britain, and represent its humiliation as a matter most easy to be achieved, betray either a mind clouded by the most irrational prejudice, or a total ignorance of human nature. However, it must be the earnest wish of every honest man never to see a trial.

—Reprinted in T.J. Stiles, editor, Founding Fathers in Their Own Words. New York: Perigee, 1999.

THINK ABOUT THIS

1. When Hamilton talks of all men having the same origin and the same right, do you think he is talking about *all* people? If not, why? Who might he believe unworthy of such rights?

2. What reasons does Hamilton give for America's eventual victory in a war with Britain?

The End of the Colonial Era:
Thomas Paine's *Common Sense*

For ten years after the hated Stamp Act, the colonies seethed and bubbled with unrest. People everywhere talked about taxation without representation and about liberty and justice. At first they did not think about the colonies becoming independent. They simply wanted a better relationship between the parent country and the colonies. They wanted Britain to give them the rights that belonged to all British subjects—or to leave them more or less alone to handle their own affairs, as it had done through most of the colonial period. But the fighting in New England in 1775 outraged King George III and made it less likely that Britain and the American colonies would be able to patch things up. Soon more and more American voices were calling for independence. None called more loudly than Thomas Paine, a soldier, thinker, and writer. In January of 1776 he published a long essay called *Common Sense*. Americans bought more than 100,000 copies of this pamphlet, which said bluntly that they faced not a disagreement over taxes but a fight for freedom. Paine's call for independence and unity among the "continentals" set the stage for what happened six months later, when the Continental Congress issued the Declaration of Independence and the colonial period came to an end.

...VOLUMES HAVE BEEN WRITTEN on the subject of the struggle between England and America. Men of all ranks have embarked in the controversy, from different motives, and with various designs; but all have been ineffectual, and the period of debate is closed. Arms, as the last resource, decide this contest. . . .

The sun never shined on a cause of greater worth. 'Tis not the affair of a city, a country, a province, or a kingdom, but of a continent—of at least one eighth part of the habitable globe. 'Tis not the concern of a day, a year, or an age; posterity are virtually involved in the contest, and will be more or less affected, even to the end of time, by the proceedings now. . . .

. . . I challenge the warmest advocate for reconciliation, to shew a single advantage that this continent can reap, by being connected with Great Britain. I repeat the challenge, not a single advantage is derived. Our corn will fetch its price in any market in Europe, and our imported goods must be paid for, buy them where we will.

. . . Everything that is right or natural pleads for separation. The blood of the slain, the weeping voice of nature cries, 'TIS TIME TO PART. Even the distance at which the almighty hath placed England and America is a strong and natural proof that the authority of the one over the other was never the design of Heaven.

. . . But where, says some, is the King of America? I'll tell you Friend, he reigns above, and doth not make havoc of mankind like the Royal— of Britain. Yet that we may not appear to be defective even in earthly honors, let a day be solemnly set apart for proclaiming a charter; let it be brought forth placed on the divine law, the word of God; let a crown be placed thereon, by which the world may know, that so far as we approve of monarchy, that in America THE LAW IS KING. . . . But lest any ill use should afterwards arise, let the crown at the conclusion of the ceremony be demolished, and scattered among the people whose right it is.

—*Reprinted in T.J. Stiles, editor,* Founding Fathers in Their Own Words.
New York: Perigee, 1999.

THINK ABOUT THIS

How does Paine use geography to support his call for independence?

Time Line

1675–1676
In King Philip's War, Indians try and fail to drive colonists out of southern New England.

1607
Jamestown, the first permanent English colony in North America, is founded in Virginia.

1663
The Carolina colony, which later splits into North and South Carolina, is founded.

1620
Pilgrims establish Plymouth colony in Massachusetts.

1664
An English fleet captures the Dutch colony of New Netherland, which becomes New York.

1636
Roger Williams from Massachusetts founds a settlement at Providence in Rhode Island; Thomas Hooker from Massachusetts founds a settlement at Hartford in Connecticut.

1632
Lord Baltimore receives grant of Maryland colony.

1630
The Puritan settlement of Massachusetts Bay colony begins. Sixteen thousand settlers arrive in the Great Migration, from 1630 to 1642.

1619
The first enslaved Africans arrive in North America, brought to Jamestown on a Dutch ship.

1679

New Hampshire, settled by colonists from Massachusetts in the 1620s, becomes independent of Massachusetts.

William Penn founds Pennsylvania colony.

1681

The British government passes a series of laws and taxes meant to raise money from the American colonies. As a result, some colonists angrily begin to call for independence.

1764–1774

1702

New Jersey colony comes under royal control.

James Oglethorpe establishes Georgia, the last of the original thirteen colonies to be founded.

1732

1703

Delaware separates from Pennsylvania to become an independent colony.

The First Continental Congress meets in Philadelphia.

1774

Battles at Lexington and Concord mark the beginning of the fight for independence

1775

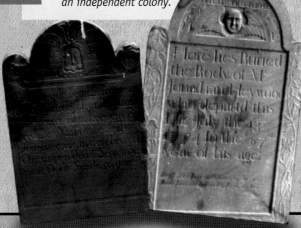

Glossary

alliance partnership between nations

annex to add new land to a nation or territory

Cataline (Lucius Sergius Catilinus) a Roman aristocrat who in 63 B.C. tried unsuccessfully to overthrow the Roman government with an army that included criminals and peasants (but not slaves)

colonize to establish settlers from a country in a place that is not part of that country

consecrated holy, dedicated to religious use

descendants of Ham black people, from a reference to the biblical character Ham, thought to be the forefather of the African race

emigrant one who emigrates, or leaves his or her homeland to live somewhere else

glyster medicine given to a patient as an enema

immigrant one who immigrates, or enters a country from somewhere else

investor one who puts money into a business or other venture in the hope of earning profits

missionary one who works to convert others to his or her religion

navigator one skilled in plotting a course and guiding a ship or other craft

rural having to do with the country rather than towns or cities; having a scattered population without town centers

To Find Out More

BOOKS

Beller, Susan Provost. *Letters from the Homefront: The Revolutionary War.* New York: Benchmark Books, 2002.

Collier, Christopher. *The Paradox of Jamestown, 1585–1700.* New York: Benchmark Books, 1998.

Cooke, Jacob Ernest, and Milton M. Klein, editors. *North America in Colonial Times: An Encyclopedia for Students.* 4 volumes. New York: Scribner's, 1998.

Dean, Ruth. *Life in the American Colonies.* San Diego: Lucent, 1999.

Fradin, Dennis. *The Thirteen Colonies.* Chicago: Childrens Press, 1988.

Hakim, Joy. *Making Thirteen Colonies,* second edition. New York: Oxford University Press, 1999.

Howarth, Sarah. *Colonial People.* Highland Park, NJ: Millbrook Press, 1994.

_____. *Colonial Places.* Highland Park, NJ: Millbrook Press, 1994.

Ingraham, Leonard. *An Album of Colonial America.* New York: Franklin Watts, 1969.

Kallen, Stuart. *Life in the Thirteen Colonies 1650–1750.* Minneapolis, MN: Abdo & Daughters, 1990.

King, David C. *Colonial Days: Discover the Past with Fun Projects, Games, Activities, and Recipes.* New York: Wiley, 1998.

Lukes, Bonnie L. *Colonial America.* San Diego: Lucent, 2000.

Maestro, Betsy. *The New Americans: Colonial Times, 1620–1689.* New York: Lothrop, Lee & Shepard, 1998.

McGovern, Ann. *If You Lived in Colonial Times.* New York: Scholastic, 1992.

Reische, Diana. *Founding the American Colonies.* New York: Franklin Watts, 1989.

Smith, Carter, editor *Daily Life: A Sourcebook on Colonial America.* Brookfield, CT: Millbrook, 1991.

———. *Explorers and Settlers: A Sourcebook on Colonial America*. Brookfield, CT: Millbrook, 1991.

Warner, John. *Colonial American Home Life*. New York: Franklin Watts, 1993.

Washburne, Carolyn K. *A Multicultural Portrait of Colonial Life*. New York: Marshall Cavendish, 1994.

WEBSITES

The websites listed here were in existence in 2000–2001 when this book was being written. Their names or locations may have changed since then.

In general, when using the Internet to do research on a history topic, you should always use caution. You will find numerous websites that are very attractive to look at and appear to be professional in format. Proceed with caution, however. Many, even the best ones, contain errors. Some websites even insert disclaimers or warnings about mistakes that may have made their way into the site. In the case of primary sources, the builders of the website often transcribe previously published material, good or bad, accurate or inaccurate. Therefore, you have to judge the content of *all* websites. This requires a critical eye.

A good rule for using the Internet as a resource is always to compare what you find in websites to several other sources, such as librarian- or teacher-recommended reference works and major works of scholarship. By doing this, you will discover the myriad versions of history that exist.

www.history.org/almanack.htm is the online Historical Almanack of Colonial Williamsburg, a Virginia exhibit of a colonial-style town. The site offers a collection of resources about colonial life for students and teachers.

www7.bcity.com/history is the Colonial American Gazette, a set of articles on a wide variety of topics in colonial history, including the formation of each colony and the roles of women and African Americans.

falcon.jmu.edu/~ramseyil/colonial.htm is the website of Colonial America 1600–1775. Resources for students at all levels, with hundreds of links to articles and educational sites on everything from colonial cooking to maps and military histories of the period.

Index

ABOUT THE AUTHOR

Rebecca Stefoff has written many books about American history, including *The Colonies* in her North American Historical Atlases series (Benchmark Books, 2001) and a biography of William Penn, founder of the Pennsylvania colony (Chelsea House, 1998). Although she now makes her home in Portland, Oregon, she formerly lived in Philadelphia, in the heart of a neighborhood that dates back to colonial times.